WEATHER
AND CLIMATE

McGRAW-HILL

SCIENCE

MACMILLAN/McGRAW-HILL EDITION

WEATHER AND CLIMATE

RICHARD MOYER ■ LUCY DANIEL ■ JAY HACKETT

PRENTICE BAPTISTE ■ PAMELA STRYKER ■ JOANNE VASQUEZ

NATIONAL
GEOGRAPHIC
SOCIETY

**McGraw-Hill
School Division**

New York   Farmington

PROGRAM AUTHORS

Dr. Lucy H. Daniel
*Teacher, Consultant
Rutherford County Schools,
North Carolina*

Dr. Jay Hackett
*Emeritus Professor of Earth
Sciences
University of Northern
Colorado*

Dr. Richard H. Moyer
*Professor of Science
Education
University of Michigan-
Dearborn*

Dr. H. Prentice Baptiste
*Professor of Curriculum and
Instruction
New Mexico State
University*

Pamela Stryker, M.Ed.
*Elementary Educator and
Science Consultant
Eanes Independent School
District
Austin, Texas*

JoAnne Vasquez, M.Ed.
*Elementary Science
Education Specialist
Mesa Public Schools,
Arizona
NSTA President 1996–1997*

NATIONAL
GEOGRAPHIC
SOCIETY

Washington, D.C.

CONTRIBUTING AUTHORS

Dr. Thomas Custer

Dr. James Flood

Dr. Diane Lapp

Doug Llewellyn

Dorothy Reid

Dr. Donald M. Silver

CONSULTANTS

Dr. Danny J. Ballard

Dr. Carol Baskin

Dr. Bonnie Buratti

Dr. Suellen Cabe

Dr. Shawn Carlson

Dr. Thomas A. Davies

Dr. Marie DiBerardino

Dr. R. E. Duhrkopf

Dr. Ed Geary

Dr. Susan C. Giarratano-Russell

Dr. Karen Kwitter

Dr. Donna Lloyd-Kolkin

Ericka Lochner, RN

Donna Harrell Lubcker

Dr. Dennis L. Nelson

Dr. Fred S. Sack

Dr. Martin VanDyke

Dr. E. Peter Volpe

Dr. Josephine Davis Wallace

Dr. Joe Yelderman

Invitation to Science, *World of Science*, and *FUNtastic Facts* features found in this textbook were designed and developed by the National Geographic Society's Education Division.

Copyright © 2000 National Geographic Society

The name "National Geographic Society" and the Yellow Border Rectangle are trademarks of the Society, and their use, without prior written permission, is strictly prohibited.

Cover Photo: *bkgnd.* © Paul Chesley/TSI; *inset* images copyright © 1998 PhotoDisc, Inc.

McGraw-Hill School Division
A Division of The McGraw-Hill Companies

Copyright © 2000 McGraw-Hill School Division,
a Division of the Educational and Professional
Publishing Group of The McGraw-Hill Companies, Inc.

McGraw-Hill School Division
Two Penn Plaza
New York, New York 10121

Printed in the United States of America

ISBN 0-02-278224-9 / 5

1 2 3 4 5 6 7 8 9 042/046 05 04 03 02 01 00 99

CONTENTS

UNIT 2 WEATHER AND CLIMATE

REFERENCE SECTION

UNIT 2

WEATHER AND CLIMATE

CHAPTER 3

WEATHER

Weather is all around you. It affects you every day. Weather can affect how you feel. It can also affect the plans you've made.

In Chapter 3 you'll explore what makes up the weather. For example, why do some clouds give us rain or snow, while others just float overhead? Why do clouds form?

 In Chapter 3 you will read to find the main idea and details that support the main idea.

Topic
EARTH SCIENCE
1

WHY IT MATTERS

Many things affect how hot it can get.

SCIENCE WORDS

insolation the amount of the Sun's energy that reaches Earth at a given time and place

atmosphere the blanket of gases that surrounds Earth

troposphere the layer of the atmosphere closest to Earth's surface

air pressure the force put on a given area by the weight of the air above it

weather what the lower atmosphere is like at any given place and time

barometer a device for measuring air pressure

Atmosphere and Air Temperature

Is it always hot everywhere in summer? Vacationers in the heart of Africa on a July day might see lions snoozing in the afternoon heat. On the same day, tourists huddled on a cruise ship in Alaska might be watching seals play near icy glaciers. How can two places on Earth have such different temperatures?

EXPLORE

HYPOTHESIZE How does the angle at which the Sun's energy hits Earth affect the warming of Earth? Write a hypothesis in your *Science Journal*. Set up an experiment to test your ideas.

Investigate if the Sun's Angle Matters

Test what factors might affect how warm an area gets.

PROCEDURES

SAFETY Do not look into the lamplight. Prop up a foam bowl, using a plate or clay, to shield your eyes from the light.

1. Place a thermometer onto each of the three blocks, as shown. Cover each with black paper. Put blocks 20 cm from the bulb, level with its filament (curly wire).

2. OBSERVE Measure the starting temperature at each block. Record the temperatures in your *Science Journal.*

3. PREDICT What will happen when the lamp is turned on? Turn the lamp on. Record the temperature at each block every two minutes, for ten minutes.

4. COMMUNICATE Make a line graph showing the change in temperature at each block over time.

5. USE VARIABLES Repeat the activity with white paper.

MATERIALS
- 3 thermometers
- triangular blocks
- black paper
- white paper
- centimeter ruler
- scissors
- tape
- 150-W clear bulb lamp
- stopwatch
- foam bowl
- clay
- *Science Journal*

CONCLUDE AND APPLY

1. COMMUNICATE Which block's surface was warmed most by the lamplight? Which block's surface was warmed the least?

2. INFER How does the angle at which light hits a surface affect how much the surface is heated? How does the surface color affect how much it is heated?

GOING FURTHER: Problem Solving

3. EXPERIMENT What other factors might affect how much a surface is warmed by sunlight? How would you test your ideas?

Does the Angle Matter?

Where do you think you might find warm temperatures all year long? Where would you find very cold weather? As the Explore Activity shows, angles make a difference in how much the Sun warms an area. The areas around the equator are hottest. That's because the Sun's path is directly overhead at midday. In those areas the Sun's rays hit Earth at their strongest.

The areas around the North and South Poles are coldest. That's because in those areas, the Sun is lower at midday. The Sun's rays hit Earth's surface at a low angle. The strength of the rays is much weaker at this angle.

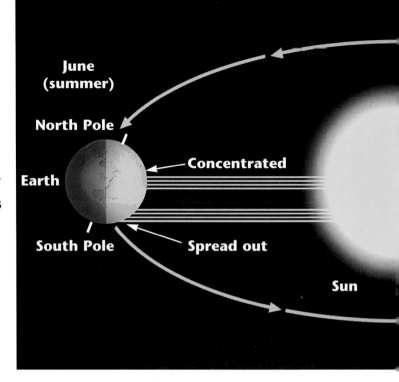

The Sun's rays strike the surface at different angles as the Earth travels around the Sun.

MONTHLY MEAN TEMPERATURE

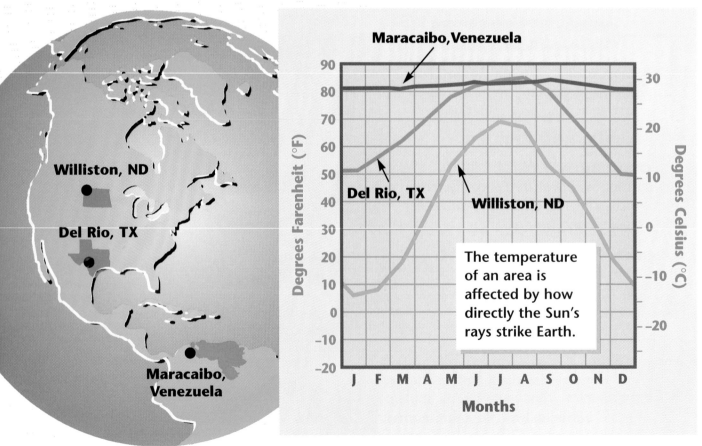

The temperature of an area is affected by how directly the Sun's rays strike Earth.

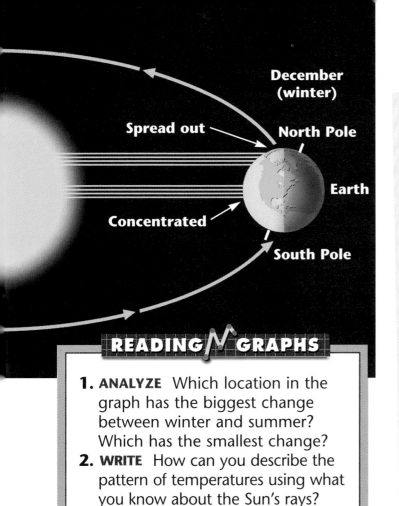

December
(winter)

Spread out

North Pole

Earth

Concentrated

South Pole

READING /\/ GRAPHS

1. **ANALYZE** Which location in the graph has the biggest change between winter and summer? Which has the smallest change?
2. **WRITE** How can you describe the pattern of temperatures using what you know about the Sun's rays?

Angles and Light

The angle at which sunlight strikes Earth's surface is so important, it is given a specific name. It is called the angle of **insolation**. *Insolation* is short for *incoming solar radiation*. It means the amount of the Sun's energy that reaches Earth at a given place and time.

The diagram shows how sunlight warms Earth in summer and winter. The amount of warming depends on the angle of insolation. The greater the angle, the warmer it gets. The angle of insolation is always smaller near the poles than near the equator. That means while it's freezing cold in one part of the world, it's hot and humid in another. How does Earth's position in its path around the Sun affect the angle of insolation where you live?

Investigating Angles

HYPOTHESIZE Why does the angle of insolation cause a difference in warming? Write a hypothesis in your *Science Journal.*

MATERIALS
- flashlight
- sheet of graph paper
- modeling clay
- 3 toothpicks
- ruler
- *Science Journal*

PROCEDURES

1. Fold a sheet of graph paper lengthwise in three equal parts. Put a small lump of clay in the middle of each part. Stand a toothpick straight up in each lump of clay.

2. Hold a flashlight directly over the first toothpick. Have a partner trace a line around the circle of light and trace the toothpick shadow.

3. **USE VARIABLES** Repeat step 2 for the other two toothpicks, changing only the angle of the flashlight.

4. **MEASURE** Count the number of boxes in each circle. Measure the lengths of the toothpick shadows. Record results in your *Science Journal.*

CONCLUDE AND APPLY

1. **INFER** How is the length of the shadows related to the angle?

2. **INFER** How is the number of boxes in the circle related to the angle?

What Has the Time Got to Do with It?

In the morning the Sun is close to the horizon. What happens as time goes by? By noon the Sun is high up in the sky, as high as it gets during the day. After noon the Sun is lower and lower in the sky.

How does this affect the angle of insolation? How do we measure it? In an earlier illustration, you saw that both location and time of year affect this angle. This illustration shows how the time of day affects the angle of insolation.

Measuring the angle of insolation is a challenge. It is not easy to see indi-vidual light rays. How can you tell if they are hitting a surface directly? Look at the shadows cast by objects they strike! The less direct the light rays, the longer the shadows. As you can see in the diagram, the angle of insolation is the same as the angle between the ground and the line from the tip of the shadow to the top of the wall.

Brain Power

Why do many coolers have smooth, light-colored surfaces? What kinds of surfaces would you use to keep things warm?

MATH LINK — ANGLE OF INSOLATION

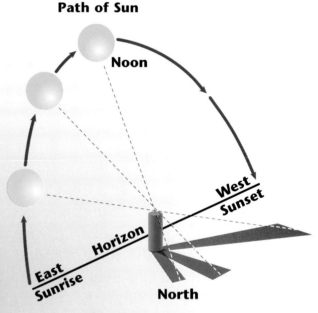

The angle of insolation can be measured by examining the angles created by shadows.

Sun's ray

Wall

Tip of shadow

Angle of insolation

Ground

30°

30°

Shadow of wall

Path of Sun

Noon

West Sunset

Horizon

East Sunrise

North

The higher the Sun is in the sky, the shorter the shadow.

READING DIAGRAMS

1. **DISCUSS** How can you measure the angle of insolation without being able to see the Sun's rays individually?
2. **WRITE** What will happen to the angle as the Sun gets higher in the sky? How will this affect the temperature?

Do Some Things Get Hotter than Others?

The Explore Activity showed that dark colors get hotter than light colors in the same light. This is why black asphalt roads get so hot in the sunlight. Dark soils and rocks also get very hot. White sand and light-colored soils do not get as hot in sunlight. Plants can also help keep an area cooler in sunlight than surrounding rocks and soil, or black asphalt.

Texture is how smooth or rough a surface is. Look at the drawing on the right. See how rough textures cause light to bounce around at many angles. Each time a little more energy is absorbed by the surface. Rough surfaces tend to get hotter in sunlight than smooth surfaces.

Why do you go swimming when it is hot and you want to cool off? Because the water is cooler than the air. The water and the land next to it are

Rough texture   Smooth texture

More impacts = more heat energy absorbed
Less impacts = less heat energy absorbed

receiving identical Sun's rays. You would expect them to be the same temperature. Why is the water cooler? Water reacts differently to light energy. As you can see in the drawing below, the same amount of light energy will heat land to a higher temperature than it will heat water.

READING GRAPHS

1. **DISCUSS** Which material is warmer after being placed near the light?
2. **DISCUSS** How can you use the graph to tell which substance heats faster?

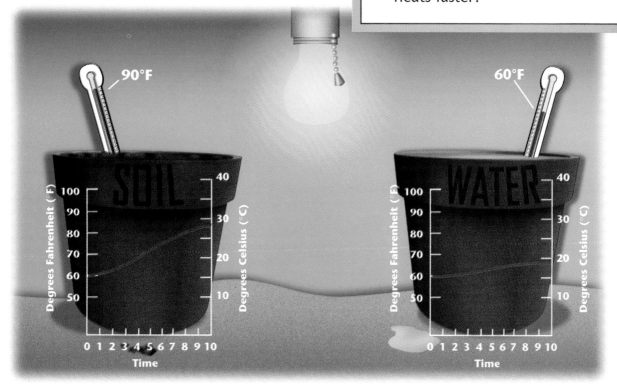

Why Do You Cool Down as You Go Up?

Did you ever climb a high mountain? As you go higher and higher above sea level, air temperatures drop. The natural drop in air temperature with altitude is about 2°C (3.6°F) for every 305 meters (1,000 ft). On a recent day in June, the air temperature in Lewiston, Maine (elevation: 34 meters [110 ft]), was a pleasant 21°C (70°F). A two-hour drive away, the air temperature at Mount Washington, New Hampshire (elevation: 1,917 meters [6,288 ft]), was a frosty 1°C (34°F).

Driving up a mountain is really a journey up into the atmosphere, the air that surrounds Earth. The atmosphere reaches from Earth's surface to the edge of space. What if you could travel to the top part of the atmosphere? The diagram of the atmosphere shows what you would find.

You would find that the temperature does not fall steadily with altitude. It changes abruptly several times. These changes mark the boundaries of four main layers. These layers surround Earth like huge shells.

The layer closest to Earth's surface is the troposphere (trop′ə sfîr′). It's the narrowest layer—between 8 and 18 kilometers (5–11 miles) thick—but it contains most of the air in the atmosphere. All life on Earth exists here. In this layer all moisture is found and all clouds, rain, snow, and thunderstorms occur. Above this layer the air gradually thins out to the near-emptiness of space, with no exact upper boundary.

THE LAYERS OF THE ATMOSPHERE

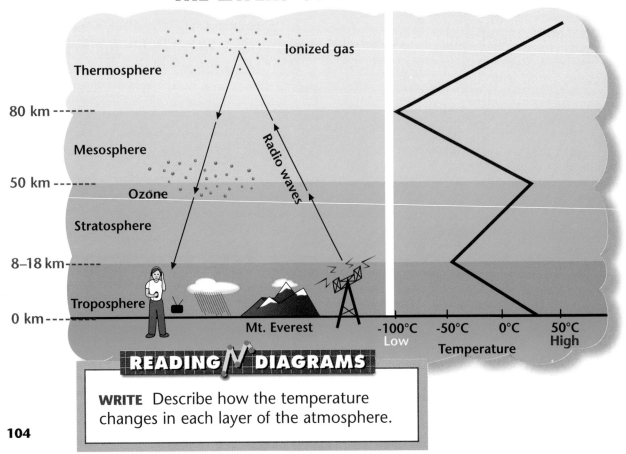

READING DIAGRAMS

WRITE Describe how the temperature changes in each layer of the atmosphere.

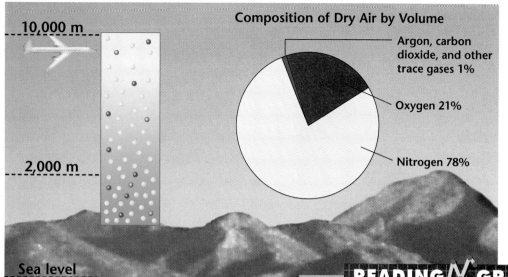

Composition of Dry Air by Volume

10,000 m

2,000 m

Sea level

Argon, carbon dioxide, and other trace gases 1%

Oxygen 21%

Nitrogen 78%

Lower altitudes have a larger air column above them which creates greater air pressure.

READING GRAPHS

1. **DISCUSS** What is meant by *trace*?
2. **WRITE** Which gas is the most abundant in the atmosphere?

What Else Happens?

As you go higher in altitude, **air pressure** decreases steadily. Air pressure is the force put on a given area by the weight of the air above it. Air is a mixture of gases. It is made up mostly of *molecules* of nitrogen and oxygen. Molecules are the smallest pieces that a substance can be broken into without changing what the substance is.

The molecules have mass. They are attracted to Earth by gravity, so they have weight.

Normal air pressure is greatest at sea level. There the column of air extending above the surface to the top of the atmosphere is tallest. Sea level air pressure is about 1.04 kilograms per square centimeter (14.7 pounds per square inch). As you go higher in altitude, the height of the air column above you becomes shorter. Therefore the weight of that column—or air pressure—becomes less.

In the lower atmosphere, the composition of air varies very little. Up to an elevation of about 100 kilometers (621 miles), air consists of a mixture of gases, water vapor, and dust particles. The gases found in pure, dry air are shown in the circle graph. Nitrogen and oxygen make up 99 percent of the gases in dry air.

Water vapor is water in the gas phase. It should not be confused with clouds or fog, which are made of liquid or solid water. The amount of water vapor in air varies from $\frac{1}{10,000}$ of air in dry arctic regions to $\frac{1}{25}$ of air in moist equatorial regions.

The dust in air is made of particles so tiny that 100,000 lined up would only form a row 1 centimeter long. Some of it comes from Earth's surface, from fires and volcanic eruptions, or from tiny crystals of salt.

What Is Weather?

When you say, "It sure is hot today!" the *it* is the air. You really mean that the air around you is hot. The same is true if you say, "It is windy, " or "It is cloudy," or give any other similar description of the weather. The weather is simply what the lower atmosphere, or troposphere, is like at any given place and time.

The conditions that make up weather are the characteristics that change. They are air temperature, air pressure, amount of moisture in the air, wind, clouds, and rain or snow.

Measuring Temperature

You can measure temperature with a thermometer. Thermometers can use two different temperature scales. The Celsius scale is marked with the letter C. The Fahrenheit scale is shown by the letter *F*.

Measuring Air Pressure

Air pressure is measured with a **barometer** (bə rom'i tər). Two common types of barometers are the mercury barometer and the aneroid barometer.

Mercury barometers use a glass tube with one closed end. The open end is submerged in liquid mercury. Air pressure on the mercury pushes it up into the tube. When the weight of the mercury column equals the air pressure, the mercury stops rising.

An *aneroid* (an'ə roid´) barometer is an accordion-like metal can with most of the air removed. Inside, a spring balances the outside air pressure. When outside air pressure increases, the can squeezes the spring. When air pressure decreases, the spring pushes outward. A needle inside indicates the changes in air pressure.

Room temperature

Freezing point

Thermometer

Aneroid barometer

These are two common types of barometers

Mercury barometer

106

How Can You Start a Weather Station?

You can monitor and record weather conditions for your own weather station. Measure and record the air temperature on both scales several times each day. If you have a barometer, you can measure and record the daily air pressure. You might also record the daily air pressure by listening to the weather reports. They often say, "The barometer reads . . . and is falling." They may say it "is rising." You will learn more about air pressure later in this chapter.

In the next few topics, you will add instruments to your weather station. Each instrument can be used to measure a different property of your local weather. By the end of the chapter, you will have a real working weather station.

Have you ever heard a day called a "scorcher"? That means a really hot day. On really hot days, your body can lose a lot of moisture. Your body gives off sweat gradually most of the time. On a hot day, your body tends to give off more and more. That's why you might consider having a bottle of water handy on a hot day.

On really cold days, many people have other problems—such as frostbite. You have to cover your face and hands to avoid contact with air at extremely low temperatures.

REVIEW

1. How do temperatures on Earth depend on angles?

2. List factors that affect temperatures of places on Earth.

3. What is air pressure? How does it change in the atmosphere?

4. **COMPARE AND CONTRAST** How are the *troposphere* and *atmosphere* alike? Different?

5. **CRITICAL THINKING** *Analyze* Is the weather one or more than just one thing? Defend your answer.

WHY IT MATTERS THINK ABOUT IT
Why is the atmosphere so important for Earth?

WHY IT MATTERS WRITE ABOUT IT
How do you depend on the weather?

NATIONAL GEOGRAPHIC

World of SCIENCE

LAYERS OF THE ATMOSPHERE

Thermosphere
From 80–700 km (50–435 mi)

Ionosphere
From 60–400 km (36–240 mi)

Mesosphere
From 50–80 km (31–50 mi)

Stratosphere
From 11–50 km (7–31 mi)

Troposphere
From 0–11 km (0–7 mi)

What's UP?

Science, Technology, and Society

Take a deep breath. Chances are you can breathe easily. That's because Earth's atmosphere contains oxygen. At sea level breathing's easy. On a mountain-top, the breathing's more difficult. Why?

In the 1600s the newly invented barometer, a device for measuring air pressure, was taken high in the mountains. There the barometer registered a lower air pressure than at sea level. The lower the air pressure, the harder it is to breathe.

Over the centuries scientists have gone even higher to investigate the layers of Earth's atmosphere. The troposphere is the layer where all life and weather occur. The troposphere begins at sea level and rises 11 kilometers (7 miles).

In the late 1800s, a scientist launched a balloon carrying a thermometer and a barometer. He discovered a warm atmospheric layer we call the stratosphere. There sunlight changes oxygen into ozone, which is why we call it the ozone layer. Ozone absorbs the Sun's radiation and keeps it from reaching Earth.

In 1901 Guglielmo Marconi sent the first radio signal across the Atlantic Ocean. The radio waves couldn't bend to follow the curvature of the Earth. Instead they were reflected back by particles, or ions, in the ionosphere.

Scientists later identified the mesosphere and thermosphere. They also discovered that some chemicals used on Earth caused a thinning of the ozone layer. Because the ozone layer protects Earth from harmful radiation, the world's nations agreed to ban the chemicals.

Air in the thermosphere is so thin that a special spacesuit is needed.

Discussion Starter

1 TV signals bounce off satellites. What does this tell you about the waves that carry TV signals?

2 When we protect the ozone layer, we protect ourselves. Why?

*inter*NET
CONNECTION To learn more about atmosphere, visit
www.mhschool.com/science and enter the keyword **SKY.**

109

Topic
EARTH SCIENCE
2

WHY IT MATTERS

The amount of water in the air can affect how you feel.

SCIENCE WORDS

water vapor water in the form of a gas

humidity the amount of water vapor in the air

evaporation the changing of a liquid into a gas

relative humidity a comparison between condensation and evaporation

condensation the changing of a gas into a liquid

Water in the Air

What if you were walking on this bridge? What would you see and feel all around you? Here's a hint. Put a cold glass of lemonade outside on a table on a hot, humid day. What do you see and feel on the outside of the glass?

What is a humid day like? You can feel a humid day. The word *humid* may make you think of moisture—fine droplets of water. Where is the moisture on a humid day?

EXPLORE

HYPOTHESIZE The lemonade glass has moisture on the side and in a puddle around the bottom. Where does the moisture come from? Is it from inside the glass? Write a hypothesis in your *Science Journal.* How might you design an experiment to test your ideas?

110

Design Your Own Experiment

WHERE DOES THE PUDDLE COME FROM?

PROCEDURES

1. EXPERIMENT Describe what you would do to test your idea about where the puddle came from. How would your test support or reject your idea?

2. COMMUNICATE Draw a diagram showing how you would use the materials. In your *Science Journal,* keep a record of your observations.

MATERIALS
- plastic drinking glasses
- ice
- paper towels
- food coloring
- thermometer
- *Science Journal*

CONCLUDE AND APPLY

1. COMMUNICATE Describe the results of your investigation.

2. COMMUNICATE What evidence did you gather? Explain what happened.

3. INFER How does this evidence support or reject your explanation?

GOING FURTHER: Problem Solving

4. USE VARIABLES Do you get the same results on a cool day as on a warm day? How might you set up an investigation to show the difference?

5. USE VARIABLES Do you get the same results on a humid day as on a dry day? How might you set up an investigation to show the difference?

Where Does the Puddle Come From?

The Explore Activity showed the water in the puddle on the table did not come from inside the glass! The water level in the glass did not drop as the puddle formed. The water in the puddle isn't lemonade. It didn't have the same color or smell.

The water in the puddle came from the air around the glass. When the warm air touched the cold glass, the air cooled. Droplets of water formed, ran down the side of the glass, and made a puddle on the table.

The water in the air is water vapor. Water vapor is water in the form of a gas. Water vapor is invisible, colorless, odorless, and tasteless. The amount of water vapor in the air is called humidity. Do not confuse humidity with droplets of liquid water you see in rain, fog, or clouds.

How does water vapor get into the air in the first place? Think about planet Earth. More than two-thirds of this planet is covered with liquid water—mostly oceans. Much of the rest—the land—has rivers, lakes, and water in the ground. The land is covered with plants. Plants also contain water. To get into the air, this liquid water must be changed into water vapor.

The changing of a liquid into a gas is called evaporation. This takes lots of energy. The main energy source for Earth is the Sun. Each day the Sun turns trillions of tons of ocean water into water vapor.

GEOGRAPHY LINK

ESTIMATE THE FRACTION AMOUNT OF THE EARTH'S WATER

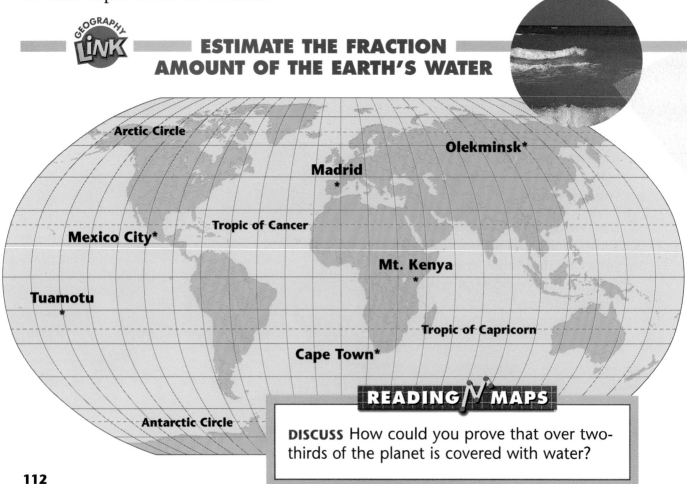

Arctic Circle

Olekminsk*

Madrid *

Mexico City*

Tropic of Cancer

Mt. Kenya *

Tuamotu *

Tropic of Capricorn

Cape Town*

Antarctic Circle

READING MAPS

DISCUSS How could you prove that over two-thirds of the planet is covered with water?

The Sun's energy gives molecules of water a "lift." Water molecules near the surface of the liquid "escape" into the atmosphere as water vapor. They move about in all directions. Some hit other molecules and return to the liquid. This is an example of condensation. Condensation is the changing of a gas into a liquid.

Plants' roots absorb water that has seeped into the ground. Plants transport the liquid water through their roots and stems to their leaves.

The leaves then give off water in the process called transpiration. This is the second-largest source of water vapor in the atmosphere.

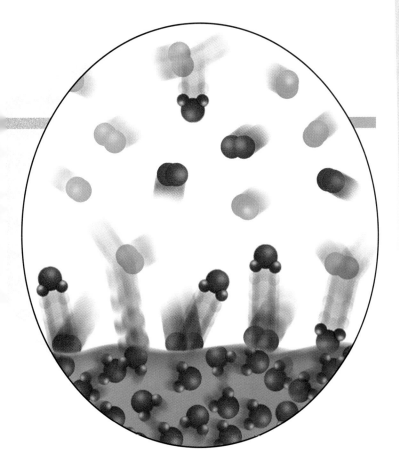

Water molecules fit between moving molecules of gas in the air. Some water molecules are knocked back into the liquid water.

QUICK LAB

Transpiration

HYPOTHESIZE What evidence can you find for transpiration? Write a hypothesis in your *Science Journal.*

MATERIALS
- potted houseplant (geraniums work well)
- transparent plastic bag
- *Science Journal*

PROCEDURES

1. Place the plastic bag completely over the plant, and secure it tightly around the base of the stem. Do not put the soil-filled pot into the bag.

2. OBSERVE Place the plant in a sunny location, and observe it several times a day. Record your observations.

3. When you are done, remove the plastic bag from the plant.

CONCLUDE AND APPLY

1. COMMUNICATE Describe what you see on the inside of the bag. Explain what happened.

2. DRAW CONCLUSIONS *Transpiration* sounds like *perspiration*—sweating. How might the two processes be alike?

3. PREDICT How would your results vary if you put the plant in the shade?

How Much Water Is in Air?

Does water just keep evaporating from a puddle, a lake, or an ocean? Yes. Does this mean the amount of water vapor in the air increases without limit? No.

One reason is condensation. As Earth's water evaporates (water molecules leave the liquid water), water vapor in the atmosphere condenses (water molecules enter the liquid water). Evaporation and condensation are opposites, and they take place at the same time.

Relative humidity is a comparison of condensation and evaporation. It is expressed as a percentage. For example, 50% means one-half. Therefore, 50% relative humidity means that the number of water molecules condensing each second is half of the number of water molecules evaporating each second.

One hundred percent relative humidity means condensation equals evaporation. This means that as many water molecules condense each second as evaporate each second. The number of water molecules in each volume of air is as high as it can be at that temperature.

Think of the amount of water vapor in a given volume of air, such as in a cubic centimeter. This amount, at 100% humidity, depends on the temperature. The reason is that the warmer the water is, the greater the evaporation. This means that the air must have a greater amount of water in it for condensation to equal evaporation. The graph shows how, at 100% humidity, the amount of water vapor per cubic centimeter changes with temperature.

READING GRAPHS

DISCUSS How does the amount of water vapor per cubic centimeter compare at 25°C and 40°C?

RELATIVE HUMIDITY

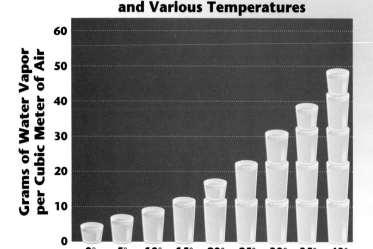

Water Vapor at 100% Humidity and Various Temperatures

Grams of Water Vapor Per Cubic Meter of Air

Temperature (°C)

Why Can Air Feel "Sticky"?

Relative humidity can be used to predict how the air will feel to a person. The higher the relative humidity, the less water can evaporate into the air. The less water, such as sweat, can evaporate from our skin, the wetter and "stickier" the air feels.

Relative humidity can also be used to predict when condensation will occur. Remember that condensation, like the drops of water on the lemonade glass, is the changing of a gas into a liquid. In the atmosphere condensation is usually the result of warm air being cooled. That is, when warm air is cooled, water vapor in it condenses.

Condensation explains what happened to the glass of lemonade. The cold glass cooled the air that touched it. Water vapor condensed, forming liquid droplets on the outside of the glass.

Can you see condensation happening? Have you ever seen frozen food held over hot water? What do you notice? You see a mist forming. When this happens in the air, a cloud forms. The greater the relative humidity, the more likely condensation will occur, and the greater the chance of clouds—and rain.

Brain Power

You may have heard people complain on a hot day, "It's not the heat, it's the humidity!" Why do you think the humidity is so important, especially when the weather is hot? Why doesn't a cold day with 70 percent humidity feel as uncomfortable as a hot day with 70 percent humidity?

Cloud forms

Warm air

1

Cloud forms

Warm air

2

The process that forms droplets of water on the lemonade glass is also the process that forms clouds—condensation.

What Happens Next?

How can warm, moist air cool off? You have learned that in the lower atmosphere, the air gets colder with increasing altitude.

- One way that air cools is by being pushed upward over mountains by winds.

- Heating of air also causes it to rise. When the ground is strongly heated by the Sun, air above the ground gets warmed and rises. It expands as it rises. As the air expands, it cools.

- Air can also be pushed upward when cooler air and warmer air meet. When the two meet, they don't mix. The lighter, warm air is pushed up over the heavier, cold air. The result is that the warm air is pushed up higher into the atmosphere, where it cools.

Whatever causes air to rise and cool, the end result is the same. As the air

rises and cools, the water vapor in it condenses into tiny water droplets, forming clouds.

If the temperature falls below the freezing point of water, its water vapor will form a cloud of tiny ice crystals.

In order for water vapor to condense, it must have a surface on which the liquid droplet or ice crystal will form. This surface is provided by the tiny dust particles that are part of the air. You will learn more about clouds in the next topic.

The glass of lemonade helped you see how several processes work. One process is evaporation. Evaporation occurs when liquid water from Earth's surface changes into a gas—water vapor. The water vapor rises and cools. Condensation takes place. Tiny droplets of water form on the glass— just as tiny droplets of water can form up in the sky and become a cloud.

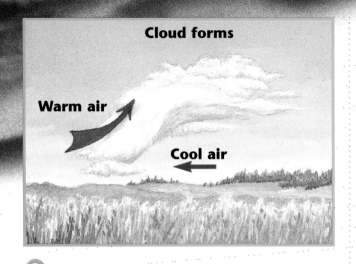

Cloud forms

Warm air

Cool air

③

READING DIAGRAMS

1. **DISCUSS** What can cause air to rise?
2. **WRITE** What happens to the air temperature as air rises?

Have you ever had sweat trickle down your face on a hot day? People sweat every day. Sweating is a way our bodies release wastes. We don't always feel the sweat because we sweat gradually and it evaporates.

As sweat evaporates, the water droplets absorb heat from the surface of the skin. This cools the skin. It is a way your body controls surface temperature.

On very hot days and when you are physically active, you may sweat a lot. The sweat builds up and does not evaporate fast enough to keep it from collecting.

On a low-humidity day, the sweat evaporates more quickly. You might think you're not sweating—but you are.

REVIEW

1. Where does water vapor in the air come from? What produces it?

2. **COMPARE AND CONTRAST** How is relative humidity different from humidity? How are the two terms alike?

3. What causes water vapor to change into droplets of liquid water?

4. How does water vapor get cooled in the atmosphere?

5. **CRITICAL THINKING** *Apply* Would you say that the Sun is a cause of clouds? Defend your answer.

WHY IT MATTERS THINK ABOUT IT
How do the two processes evaporation and condensation depend on each other? Why can't there be one without the other?

WHY IT MATTERS WRITE ABOUT IT
Why are you more comfortable when the relative humidity is low than when it is high?

Comparing Quantities

Weather forecasters express relative humidity as a percentage. Do this activity, and you'll get practice at calculating percentages.

WHAT YOU NEED

► 3 plastic glasses (small, medium, large)

► graduated cylinder

► water

WHAT TO DO

1. Fill the small glass with water. Pour it in the cylinder to determine how much water the glass holds. Record this number. Repeat with the medium and large glasses.

1. Fill the small glass with water again. What percent of its volume is filled? Record this percent.

3. Pour the water from the small glass into the medium glass. Divide the amount of water in the medium glass by the amount of water it could hold. Multiply this number by 100. This is the percent of the medium glass that's filled with water. Record this percent.

4. Refill the small glass. Now pour the water into the large glass. Find the percent of the large glass that's now filled with water. (Follow the procedure in step 3.) Record this percent.

Math Link

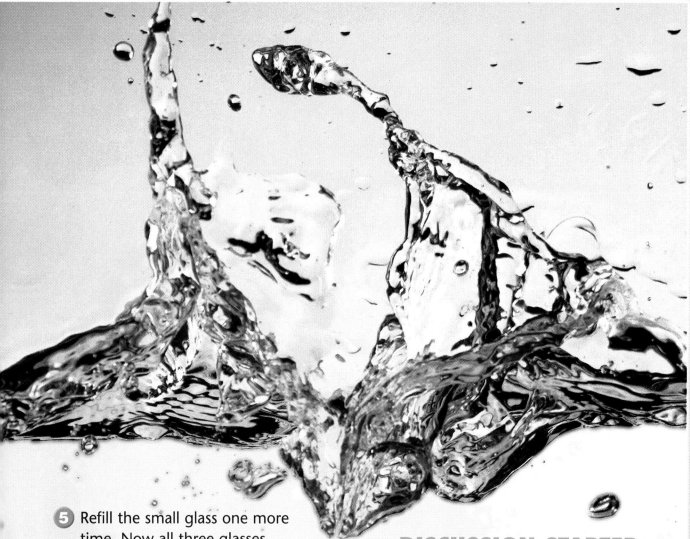

5. Refill the small glass one more time. Now all three glasses should have the same amount of water in them.

6. Apply the concept of percentages to relative humidity. Divide the rate of condensation by the rate of evaporation. Multiply by 100. The result is the relative humidity. For example, what if the rate of condensation is one-quarter the rate of evaporation? This means that the relative humidity is one divided by four ($\frac{1}{4}$) times 100, or 25%.

DISCUSSION STARTER

1. If the rate of condensation equals the rate of evaporation, then what is the relative humidity?

2. If the rate of condensaton is half the rate of evaporation, then what is the relative humidity?

To learn more about humidity, visit *www.mhschool.com/science* and enter the keyword HUMIDITY.

*inter*NET
CONNECTION

WHY IT MATTERS

Clouds, rain, snow, and hail can have great impact on crops and on us.

SCIENCE WORDS

stratus cloud a cloud that forms in a blanketlike layer

cumulus cloud a puffy cloud that appears to rise up from a flat bottom

cirrus cloud a high-altitude cloud with a featherlike shape, made of ice crystals

fog a cloud that forms at ground level

precipitation any form of water particles that falls from the atmosphere and reaches the ground

water cycle the continuous movement of water between Earth's surface and the air, changing from liquid to gas to liquid

Clouds of Water and Ice

How can you predict the weather without using the instruments weather forecasters use? Look at the sky. There are clues up there. They're called clouds. Different kinds of clouds bring different kinds of weather. What is a cloud?

EXPLORE

HYPOTHESIZE Sometimes the sky is full of clouds. Sometimes there are no clouds at all. Why? What makes a cloud form? What do evaporation and condensation have to do with it? Write a hypothesis in your *Science Journal*. How might you make a model to test your ideas?

Investigate Why Clouds Form

Watch what can happen when you cool off some air.

PROCEDURES

SAFETY Be careful handling the hot water. Use the handle to hold the mug. Do not burn yourself.

1. Chill container 1 by putting it in a refrigerator or on ice for about ten minutes.

2. Fill a mug with hot tap water.

3. **MAKE A MODEL** Fill container 2 with hot water. Place empty cold container 1 upside down on top of container 2 with the water. Fit the mouths together carefully. Place the ice cubes on top of container 1.

4. **OBSERVE** Write your observations in your *Science Journal*.

CONCLUDE AND APPLY

1. **COMMUNICATE** What did you observe?

2. **COMMUNICATE** Where did this take place?

3. **COMMUNICATE** Where did the water come from?

4. **INFER** Explain what made it happen.

GO FURTHER: Apply

5. **DRAW CONCLUSIONS** Where would you expect to find more clouds— over the ocean or over a desert? Why?

6. **INFER** Why don't all clouds look the same?

MATERIALS

- hot tap water
- 2 identical clear containers
- mug
- 3 ice cubes
- food coloring
- refrigerator or freezer
- *Science Journal*

Stratus clouds

Cumulus clouds

Cirrus clouds

Why Do Clouds Form?

What has to happen for a cloud to form? The Explore Activity was a model of how clouds form. Clouds are made up of tiny water droplets or ice crystals. The air is filled with water vapor. When the air is cooled, the water vapor condenses. That is, the water molecules clump together around dust and other particles in the air. They form droplets of water.

Clouds look different depending on what they are made of. Water-droplet clouds tend to have sharp, well-defined edges. If the cloud is very thick, it may look gray, or even black. That's because sunlight is unable to pass through. Ice-crystal clouds tend to have fuzzy, less distinct edges. They also look whiter.

Clouds are found only in the troposphere. There are three basic cloud forms. **Stratus clouds** form in blanketlike layers. **Cumulus clouds** are puffy clouds that appear to rise up from a flat bottom. **Cirrus clouds** form at very high altitudes out of ice crystals and have a wispy, featherlike shape. If rain or snow falls from a cloud, the term *nimbo*—for "rain"—is added to the cloud's name.

Clouds are further grouped into families by height and form. They are low clouds, middle clouds, high clouds, and clouds that develop upward–clouds of vertical development. Cumulonimbus clouds develop upward. These clouds bring thunderstorms. They can start as low clouds and reach up to the highest clouds.

If moist air at ground level cools, a cloud can form right there. A cloud at ground level is called **fog**.

TYPES OF CLOUDS

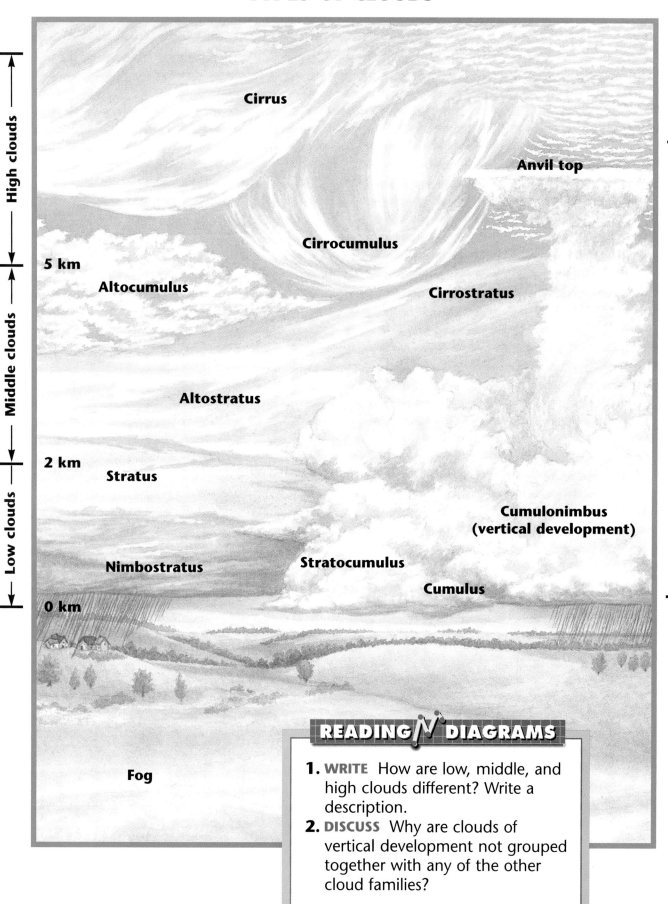

High clouds

Middle clouds

Low clouds

Clouds of vertical development

Cirrus

Anvil top

Cirrocumulus

5 km

Altocumulus

Cirrostratus

Altostratus

2 km

Stratus

Cumulonimbus
(vertical development)

Nimbostratus

Stratocumulus

Cumulus

0 km

Fog

READING N DIAGRAMS

1. **WRITE** How are low, middle, and high clouds different? Write a description.
2. **DISCUSS** Why are clouds of vertical development not grouped together with any of the other cloud families?

How Do Rain and Snow Happen?

How do rain and snow form and fall? **Precipitation** is any form of water particles that falls from the atmosphere and reaches the ground. Precipitation can be liquid (rain) or solid (such as snow).

Clouds are made up of tiny water droplets or ice crystals. They are only about $\frac{1}{50}$ of a millimeter. These tiny particles are so light that they remain "hanging" in the air. This is why many clouds do not form precipitation.

Precipitation occurs when cloud droplets or ice crystals join together and become heavy enough to fall. They clump around particles of dust in the air. Each particle is like a *nucleus* that the water molecules condense around. The chart shows the different types of precipitation and how they form.

READING N CHARTS

1. **DISCUSS** Classify the types of precipitation into two groups—solids and liquids. Explain.
2. **WRITE** Which types of precipitation form in similar ways? Explain.

TYPES OF PRECIPITATION

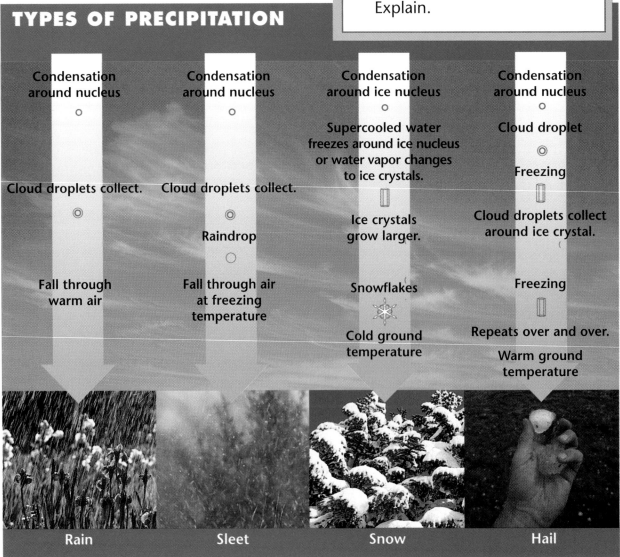

Condensation around nucleus	Condensation around nucleus	Condensation around ice nucleus	Condensation around nucleus
			Cloud droplet
		Supercooled water freezes around ice nucleus or water vapor changes to ice crystals.	Freezing
Cloud droplets collect.	Cloud droplets collect.	Ice crystals grow larger.	Cloud droplets collect around ice crystal.
	Raindrop		Freezing
Fall through warm air	Fall through air at freezing temperature	Snowflakes	Repeats over and over.
		Cold ground temperature	Warm ground temperature
Rain	**Sleet**	**Snow**	**Hail**

How Are Cloud Type and Precipitation Related?

Do certain kinds of clouds give certain kinds of precipitation? Yes.

- In tall clouds there is more chance for droplets to run into one another and combine, making larger raindrops.

- Precipitation from large cumulus clouds is often heavy rain or snow showers. However, it usually doesn't last too long.

- Precipitation from stratus clouds is usually long lasting, with smaller drops of rain or snowflakes.

- Clouds with great vertical development hold a lot of water. These clouds are very *turbulent*, or violent. Their tops often reach heights where it is below freezing. They often produce great downpours. They also sometimes produce *hail*. Hail is pellets made of ice and snow.

These clouds have updrafts—strong winds move up inside. Hail forms when updrafts in these huge clouds hurl ice crystals upward again and again. As the crystals fall, they become coated with water. As they rise the water freezes into an icy outer shell. This process usually happens over and over, adding more and more layers to the hailstones. The more violent the updrafts, the bigger the hailstone can get before it falls to the ground.

Path of Growing Hailstone

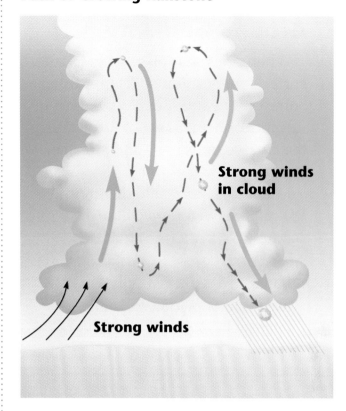

Strong winds in cloud

Strong winds

How Does Water Go Around and Around?

When precipitation reaches Earth's surface, it doesn't just disappear. Some of it evaporates right back into the atmosphere. Some of it runs off the surface into rivers and streams. We call this water *runoff*.

Much of it seeps into the ground. We call this water *groundwater*.

Groundwater collects in tiny holes, or pores, in soil and rocks. Groundwater can often seep down through soil and rocks when the pores are interconnected. It can fill up all the pores in a layer of rock below the surface. Much of this water eventually moves back to the rivers and then to lakes or oceans.

Brain Power

What kind of precipitation is most common in your area? Where does the run off go?

THE WATER CYCLE

Condensation the process in which a gas is changed to a liquid

Transpiration the process by which plant leaves release water into the air

Evaporation the process in which a liquid changes directly to a gas

Earth's water moves from place to place through the processes of evaporation, condensation, and precipitation. Condensation and precipitation take water out of Earth's atmosphere. Evaporation puts water back into the atmosphere. This complex web of changes is called the water cycle.

The water cycle is the continuous movement of water between Earth's surface and the air, changing from liquid to gas to liquid. The diagram shows the many different paths water can take into and out of the atmosphere in the water cycle.

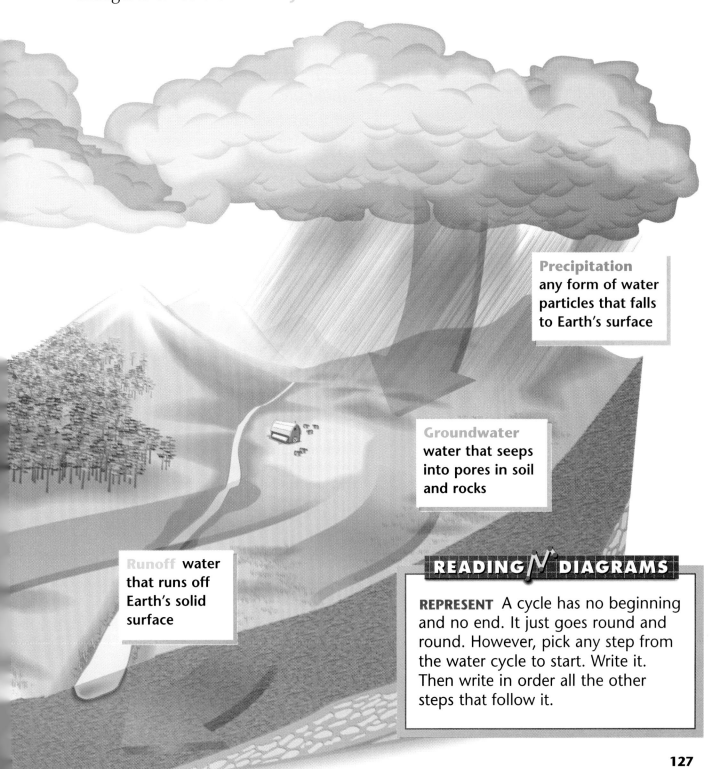

Precipitation any form of water particles that falls to Earth's surface

Groundwater water that seeps into pores in soil and rocks

Runoff water that runs off Earth's solid surface

READING N' DIAGRAMS

REPRESENT A cycle has no beginning and no end. It just goes round and round. However, pick any step from the water cycle to start. Write it. Then write in order all the other steps that follow it.

Feel the Humidity

HYPOTHESIZE Why do you feel warmer on a high humidity day? Write a hypothesis in your *Science Journal.*

MATERIALS

- 2-in.-square piece of old cotton cloth
- rubber band
- thermometer
- $\frac{1}{2}$ c of cold water
- 1 c of warm water
- *Science Journal*

PROCEDURES

SAFETY Be careful handling warm water.

1. **OBSERVE** Record the air temperature in your *Science Journal.*

2. Put thermometer in cold water. Add warm water slowly until water temperature matches air temperature.

3. Wrap cloth around bulb of thermometer. Gently hold it with a rubber band. Dampen cloth in the water.

4. **OBSERVE** Wave thermometer gently in air. Record temperatures every 30 seconds for three minutes.

CONCLUDE AND APPLY

1. **INFER** What happened to temperature of wet cloth? How does cloth feel? Explain.

2. **INFER** Suppose you try this experiment on a day that is humid and on a day that is dry. Will you get the same results? Explain.

How Do You Record How Cloudy It Is?

In Topic 1 you started your weather station. Now that you have learned about humidity and precipitation, let's add observations of these weather conditions to your weather station.

As you record weather information each day, you might record the types of clouds you see in the sky. You can use the charts in this lesson to indicate the cloud family and the types of clouds.

Try to estimate the cloud cover—that is, the amount of the sky covered by clouds. Use the terms *clear, scattered clouds, partly cloudy, mostly cloudy,* or *overcast* to describe cloud cover.

A Weather Station Model

One way to record cloud cover is to make a weather station model. Start by drawing a circle for each day. An empty circle means "clear skies." A fully shaded circle means "completely overcast." Portions of a circle are shaded to show different amounts of cloud cover.

Showing cloud cover on a weather station model.

○ Clear

● Overcast

◑ Scattered clouds

◑ Partly cloudy

◕ Mostly cloudy

How Do You Measure Rainfall?

Precipitation is measured with a rain gauge. You can make a simple rain gauge from an empty coffee can. Just place it outside, open end up. Keep it out in the open, away from buildings or trees. When the precipitation stops, measure its depth in the can. You may measure in inches with a standard ruler. If you have a metric ruler, use millimeters (the smallest unit). Keep track of the type of precipitation and how much falls.

You should also record the relative humidity. Listen to weather reports or refer to your local newspaper to obtain the relative humidity.

WHY IT MATTERS

If you ever had a baseball game rained out, you know how rain can ruin your day.

Rain may ruin your plans for a day, but rain is vital for life on Earth. Rain helps crops grow. That means food for you and others! Rain helps build the amount of water in wells and water-collecting areas, such as reservoirs. If you ever had a drought in your area, a time when there was little or no precipitation, you know how scarce water can be.

Hail on the other hand, can ruin entire crops. It can also damage cars and buildings.

REVIEW

1. How do clouds form?

2. What are some different types of precipitation? Why are there different types?

3. **SEQUENCE OF EVENTS** What are the main processes that show how liquid water changes in the water cycle? List the parts in order to show the changes.

4. How can you measure and describe the amount of precipitation and cloud cover on a given day?

5. **CRITICAL THINKING** *Apply* "Sun showers" are sudden rainfalls on a sunny day. How can a sun shower happen?

WHY IT MATTERS **THINK ABOUT IT**
What are some things you do that need a sunny day—or at least a day without precipitation? What do you do if it rains or snows?

WHY IT MATTERS **WRITE ABOUT IT**
If there was a drought in your area, what would you do to cut back on using water?

Flood: Good News or Bad?

Can you imagine a flood being good news? It was to many ancient Egyptians living near the Nile River. They looked forward to its annual summer flood. Land that was flooded was better for crops!

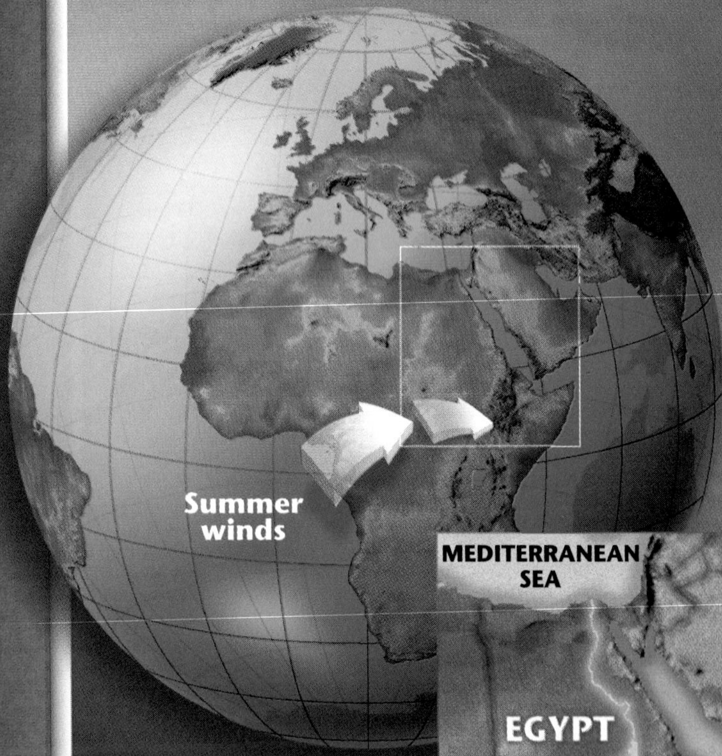

The flood wasn't all good news. Buildings and fences were swept away. Landowners had to hire "rope stretchers" to mark their property lines again.

No one knew for sure why the flood came. People believed that great rains fell near the source of the Nile to start the flood. It actually started in the mountains of Ethiopia!

Ethiopia has many mountains over 4,000 meters (13,000 feet) tall. In June the monsoons blow from the South Atlantic over the rain forests of Africa. When the winds reach the mountains of Ethiopia, giant rain clouds let loose their water in great thunderstorms. Rain-filled mountain streams join to form a great river. It carries the water to the Nile. By July the water reaches Egypt and produces the flood.

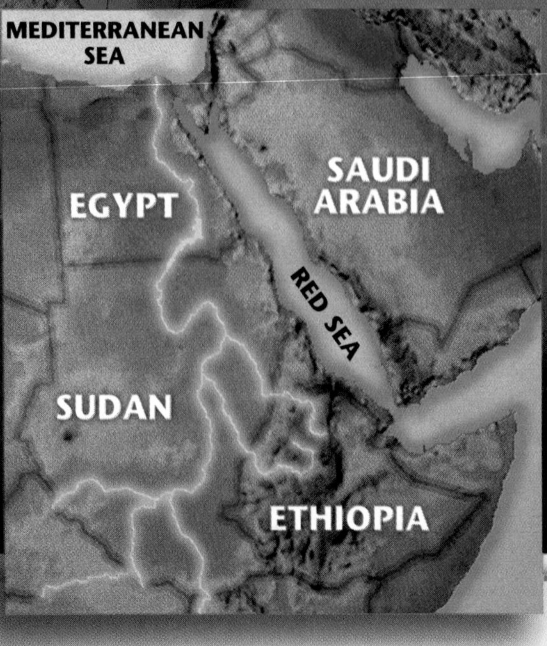

Summer winds

MEDITERRANEAN SEA

EGYPT

SAUDI ARABIA

RED SEA

SUDAN

ETHIOPIA

Today the flood waters are stopped soon after they reach Egypt. A high dam holds back the water to form a great lake. The good news is that buildings on the shore are no longer swept away. Fences mark boundaries, and instead of one crop a year, farmers plant two.

Stopping the flood has changed the environment, and that's bad news. The flood kept the fields fertile; but now farmers must use fertilizer. The Mediterranean was nourished by mud from the Nile. Now fish that were common are gone, and a serious disease is spread by snails thriving in the Nile's slow waters.

DISCUSSION STARTER

1. A dry canyon has a FLOOD DANGER sign. How could the canyon flood when no rain is falling near the sign?

2. Straightening a river can stop flooding. Why? What are the disadvantages of doing it?

To learn more about floods, visit *www.mhschool.com/science* and enter the keyword OVERFLOW.

*inter*NET
CONNECTION

WHY IT MATTERS

Wind results from differences in air pressure. Wind can be destructive but is often quite useful.

SCIENCE WORDS

wind air that moves horizontally

convection cell a circular pattern of air rising, air sinking, and wind

sea breeze wind that blows from sea to land

land breeze wind that blows from land to sea

Coriolis effect the curving of the path of a moving object caused by Earth's rotating

isobar a line on a weather map connecting places with equal air pressure

wind vane a device that indicates wind direction

anemometer a device that measures wind speed

Air Pressure and Wind

What makes the air move? Air is almost always on the move. Sometimes it's huge country-sized masses of air that are moving. Sometimes it's small patches. You've felt moving air. It's called wind. Some winds move so fast and powerfully, they can knock down trees or even lift trucks into the air. Winds move these balloons. Winds can be so gentle, they hardly ruffle your hair. Strong or weak, what makes winds blow?

EXPLORE

HYPOTHESIZE Air moves from one place to another because of differences in air pressure. What causes these differences? Write a hypothesis in your *Science Journal*. Make a model to test your ideas.

Investigate What Can Change Air Pressure

Put the atmosphere in a jar to explore air pressure.

PROCEDURES

1. MAKE A MODEL Set up a jar-and-bag system as shown. Make sure the masking tape covers the hole in the jar. Have a partner place both hands on the jar and hold it firmly. Reach in and slowly pull up on the bottom of the bag. In your *Science Journal,* describe what happens.

2. EXPERIMENT Pull the small piece of tape off the hole in the bottom of the jar. Repeat step 1. Push in on the bag. Record results in your *Science Journal.*

3. OBSERVE Place some small bits of paper on the table. Hold the jar close to the table. Point the hole toward the bits of paper. Pull up on the bag, and observe and record what happens.

4. EXPERIMENT Do just the opposite. Push the bag back into the jar, and observe. What happened?

CONCLUDE AND APPLY

1. COMPARE AND CONTRAST What differences did you observe with the hole taped and with the tape removed?

2. INFER Explain what happened each time you pushed the bag back into the jar. Why did it happen?

3. DRAW CONCLUSIONS How does this model show air pressure changes?

GOING FURTHER: Problem Solving

4. USE VARIABLES Will the model work the same with paper clips? Bits of cotton? Rubber pads? Make a prediction, and test it.

MATERIALS

- plastic jar with hole in bottom
- plastic sandwich bag
- rubber band
- masking tape
- *Science Journal*

Step 1

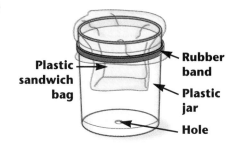

Plastic sandwich bag · Rubber band · Plastic jar · Hole

How Can Air Pressure Change?

Many factors can affect the air pressure of a region. Here are some of those factors.

Volume

Pulling up on the bag in the Explore Activity increases the volume inside the bag-jar system. The amount of air inside stays the same. The air inside the jar spreads out into the larger volume. The air pressure inside the bag-jar becomes less. The outside air pushes in harder than the inside air pushes out. That extra force pushing in is what you pull against as you pull up on the bag.

Height Above Earth's Surface

Air pressure depends on the weight of its molecules pressing down on a given area. Molecules are closer together, or more dense, at sea level than high in the atmosphere. Denser air weighs more than an equal volume of less dense air and pushes down harder. That is why air pressure is higher at sea level than high in the atmosphere.

Temperature

Air pressure also depends on temperature. When air is heated, its molecules speed up. The faster-moving molecules move around more. They spread out into a larger space. Thus the same volume of air weighs less, and the pressure decreases. What do you think happens when air is cooled?

AN AIR PRESSURE MODEL

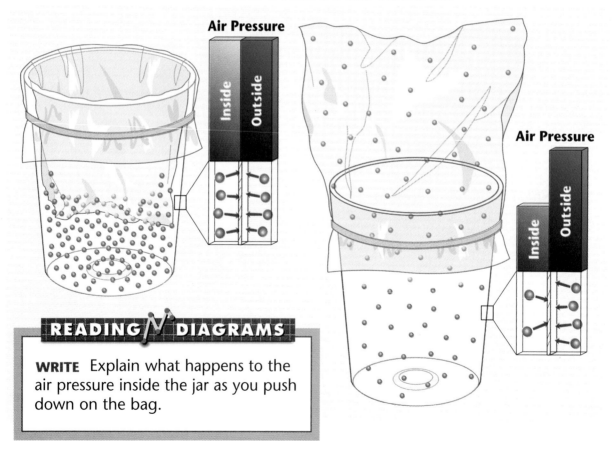

Air Pressure

Inside Outside

Air Pressure

Inside Outside

READING DIAGRAMS

WRITE Explain what happens to the air pressure inside the jar as you push down on the bag.

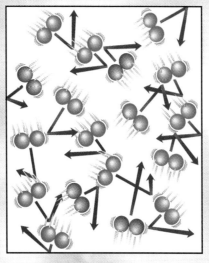

Cold air

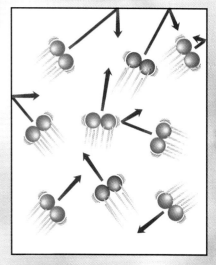

Warm air

Even though the molecules are moving slower and collide with less force, the cold air on the left exerts more pressure because its closely spaced molecules collide much more frequently.

READING N DIAGRAMS

WRITE What differences do you see between the pictures for cold air and warm air?

Amount of Water Vapor

Air is a mixture of nitrogen, oxygen, and other gases. Adding water vapor to air also affects air pressure. Molecules of oxygen or nitrogen are heavier than molecules of water vapor. Light molecules exert less pressure because they weigh less. In moist air lighter water vapor molecules take the place of heavier oxygen and nitrogen molecules. Thus moist air exerts less pressure than dry air.

Air Pressure on a Station Model

You can now enter two more bits of information on your weather station model. To the upper right, place the air pressure reading in millibars. Right below this number, you may wish to put a short line. This line tells how air pressure is changing at that station.

- A line slanting to the upper right indicates the air pressure is rising (a rising

barometer). A rising barometer may be a sign that fair weather is approaching.

- A line slanting to the lower right tells the air pressure is falling (a falling barometer). A falling barometer may be a sign that a storm is on its way.

- A horizontal line indicates the air pressure is not changing. In the station model, the air pressure is 980 millibars and is rising.

Showing Air Pressure on a Station Model

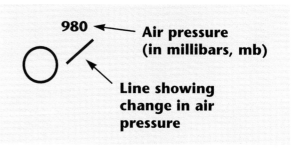

980 ← Air pressure (in millibars, mb)

Line showing change in air pressure

Why Do Winds Blow from High to Low?

Think of what happens if you put a blob of soft clay on a table and push down on it, using a flat hand. The putty squishes out from under your fingers, where the pressure is high. It moves to the spaces between your fingers, where the pressure is lower.

Air acts in a similar way. Denser air exerts a higher pressure than less dense air. Like the putty, denser air flows toward less dense air. This flow of air is wind. Air that moves horizontally is called wind. Air that rises or sinks is an *updraft* or a *downdraft*.

Convection Cells

How can air become more or less dense? As the Sun's rays hit an area, it transfers energy to the air. The air heats up. Because it is warmer, the heated air is less dense. Then, just like a cork in water, the warm air rises above the surrounding cooler, denser air. On the other hand, if a region of air is cooled, it becomes denser and sinks.

This unequal heating and cooling of the air often makes a pattern of rising air, sinking air, and winds, called a **convection** (kən vek′shən) **cell**. A convection cell is a part of the atmosphere where air moves in a circular pattern because of unequal heating and cooling.

The drawing shows how a convection cell forms. Cities A and B have the same air pressure. Then direct sunlight heats city A. The air above it warms and expands. It becomes less dense and rises, forming an updraft. The air pressure goes down. The unheated air on either side has a higher pressure. This air moves in toward the low-pressure area, making a surface wind.

READING ✓ DIAGRAMS

DISCUSS Use the diagram to explain what happens to city B during the formation of the convection cell.

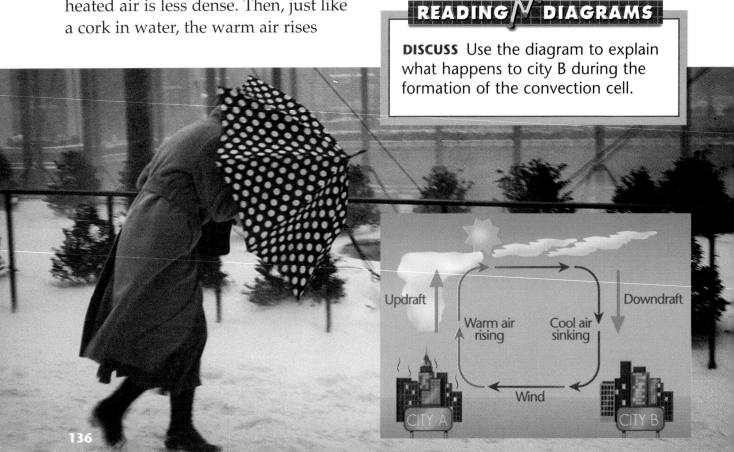

Updraft · Downdraft · Warm air rising · Cool air sinking · Wind · CITY A · CITY B

Warm air

Cold air

Sea breeze

Warm air

Cold air

Valley breeze

What Are Sea and Land Breezes?

An example of convection is a breeze that occurs along a coastline. In Topic 1 you learned that land warms faster than water. On sunny days air over land warms faster than air next to it over the sea. The warm air expands and rises. Cooler air from over the ocean replaces the rising warm air. A wind blows onto the land. A wind that blows from the sea toward the land is called a sea breeze.

At night the reverse happens. The air over the land cools more rapidly than the air over the water. A land breeze blows from land toward the water.

Convection cells also occur along mountains. As the Sun shines on a mountain during the day, the slope heats up faster than the valley below. Air over the mountain slope warms

READING DIAGRAMS

REPRESENT These pictures show what happens during the day. How would you show what happens at night?

and rises. Cooler air over the valley replaces the rising warm air. This causes a wind called a *valley breeze* to blow up the slope. At night the mountain slope cools rapidly. The air over the mountain slope is colder than the air over the valley. This causes a wind called a *mountain breeze* to blow down the slope.

137

What Is the Coriolis Effect?

Earth's rotation affects winds blowing across its surface. As Earth rotates, every spot on its surface moves with it. However, in the same 24-hour period, places near the poles travel a shorter distance than places near the equator. This means that places near the poles are moving slower!

Now what if you are in an airplane flying in a straight line from the North Pole to Chicago? While you are in the air, Earth is *rotating*, or spinning, underneath you. Earth rotates counterclockwise as seen from the North Pole. As Earth rotates, Chicago is moving west to east. To someone in Chicago, though, the plane's flight path seems to curve to the southwest.

The same thing happens with winds blowing from the North Pole. Because Earth spins, the winds seem to curve to the right as they head southward.

No matter which way the wind blows, it will curve to the right in the Northern Hemisphere. This curving is called the **Coriolis effect**. In the Southern Hemisphere, the Coriolis effect causes winds to curve to the left. This is because, as viewed from the South Pole, Earth rotates clockwise. The effect works on other moving objects as well, such as missiles and rockets.

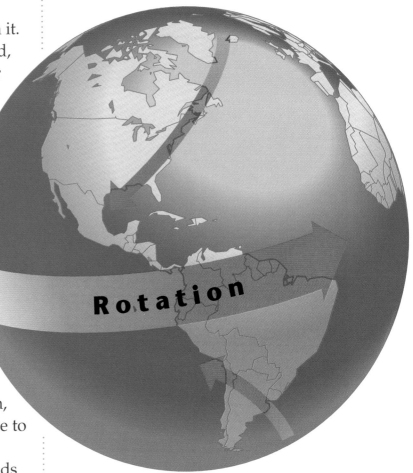

If you were standing at the North Pole looking south, this arrow would appear to curve to the right.

If you were standing at the South Pole looking north, this arrow would appear to curve to the left.

Brain Power

The Coriolis effect causes winds in the Northern Hemisphere to curve to the right. Does it also cause changes in ocean currents? How? Find an example on a globe.

How Are Wind Patterns Produced Globally?

Year round the equator is heated strongly by sunlight. The air becomes very warm. Heat also causes evaporation, so the air becomes moist. Warm, moist air over the equator creates a zone of low pressure that circles the globe.

As the air at the equator warms, it becomes less dense and rises. It rises to the top of the troposphere and spreads out, moving north and south. As the air moves away from the equator, it cools and becomes denser. At about 30° north and south latitudes, the cold air begins to sink toward the surface. This sinking air creates a high-pressure zone on both sides of the equator at these latitudes. A belt of winds is set in motion around Earth by air moving from these high-pressure zones toward the low pressure at the equator. These are the *trade winds*. The Coriolis effect curves these winds as you see in the diagram.

The poles get very indirect sunlight, and the air there is very cold. Cold, dense air can hold very little water vapor. Cold, dry air over the poles has high pressure. Air at the poles moves toward 60° latitude, forming winds. Because of the Coriolis effect, the winds curve. These are the polar *easterly winds*. *Easterly* means the wind blows "from the east."

Other winds occur between 60° latitude and the poles as well as between 30° and 60° latitudes. Between 30° and 60° latitudes is the zone of *westerly winds*. The continental United States is in the zone of westerly winds.

GEOGRAPHY LINK GLOBAL WIND ZONES

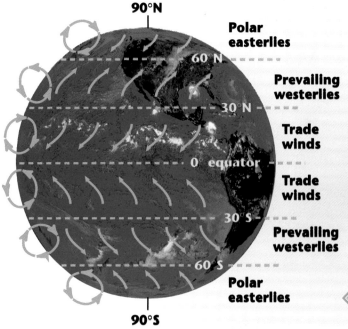

90°N

Polar easterlies

60 N

Prevailing westerlies

30 N

Trade winds

0 equator

Trade winds

30 S

Prevailing westerlies

60 S

Polar easterlies

90°S

READING DIAGRAMS

REPRESENT Make a table listing different global wind zones and a description of the directions in which winds move in each zone.

Can You Predict How Air Will Move?

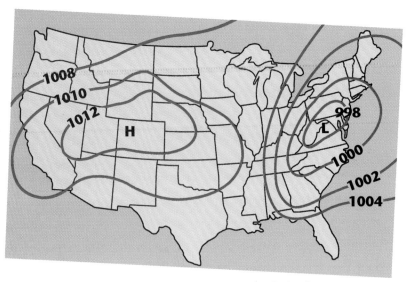

The pressure on each isobar is labeled in millibars (mb).

Why is it important to know about air pressure? Knowing where the air pressure is high or low allows you to predict which way air will move. This is why weather scientists make maps showing air pressure. They start by plotting the air pressure at many different locations on a map. Then they connect all places with the same air pressure with a line. A line on a map connecting places with equal air pressure is called an **isobar**. Isobars make pressure patterns easier to see.

Do you see the series of circular isobars in the west, surrounding a region of high pressure? This pattern is called a *high-pressure system*. Since the center has higher pressure than its surroundings, winds blow outward from the center in a clockwise pattern.

A similar set of isobars in the east marks a *low-pressure system*. In a low-pressure system, the central region is surrounded by higher pressure. The winds blow in toward the center. This time the winds blow in a counterclockwise pattern.

Isobars also help scientists predict how fast air will move. Big differences in air pressure over short distances cause strong winds. This is shown on a map by drawing closely spaced isobars. Small differences in air pressure cause gentle winds. This is shown by widely spaced isobars.

Wind on a Station Model

You show wind on a station model by a straight line touching the circle. The line tells where the wind is blowing from. "Feathers" are used to show speed.

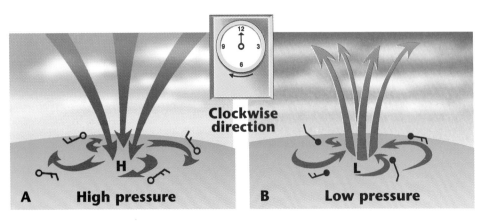

Clockwise direction

A   High pressure

B   Low pressure

Showing Wind on a Station Model

NE = Northeast wind

Half feather = 5 – 13 km/h (3 – 7 knots)

Full feather = 14 – 22 km/h (8 – 12 knots)

Skills: Using Numbers and Interpreting Data

A WEATHER STATION MODEL

A weather station model shows the weather at one weather station. A station model includes temperature, cloud cover, air pressure, pressure tendency, wind speed, and wind direction. The circle is at the location of the station. The temperature may be recorded.

MATERIALS
- *Science Journal*

Wind direction (from north) Wind speed (knots or km/h)

Air temperature (°C) (It may also be recorded in °F.) 13 | 1014 Air pressure (mb)

Pressure change

Cloud cover

PROCEDURES

1. **USE NUMBERS** Look carefully at the first weather station model. How fast is the wind blowing? What is the wind direction? Record your answers in your *Science Journal*.

2. **USE NUMBERS** What other information does the first weather station model give you?

34 ◯ 1004
Dallas

28 ◑ 980
Charlotte

14 ◔ 1012
Oakland

30 ◑ 996
Tampa

3. Look at the weather station models of the other cities. Make a table in your *Science Journal*. In your table record the weather conditions for each city.

CONCLUDE AND APPLY

1. **EVALUATE** Compare the information in the table you made with these station models. Which way is the information easier to interpret?

2. **COMPARE AND CONTRAST** Where was wind the fastest? The slowest? Which tells you this information more quickly, the chart or your models?

3. **COMPARE AND CONTRAST** Compare and contrast other weather conditions in the cities. Tell which is the "most" or "least" for each condition.

How Do We Determine Wind Direction and Speed?

What do the roofs on the right have in common? Each has a curious-looking device on the roof. Did you know that each of these is a wind vane? A wind vane is used to tell wind direction. A wind vane has a pointer that blows around in the wind. The pointer is mounted so it can point to the different compass markings.

The tail of the pointer has a larger surface area than the tip. When a wind blows, it exerts more pressure on the tail than the tip. This causes the tail to swing around so that the tip points in the direction the wind is blowing from.

By looking at the compass markings, you can tell which direction the wind is blowing from. Can you tell the tip from the tail in each of the wind vanes shown?

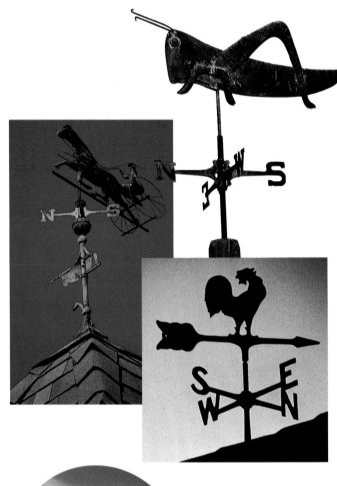

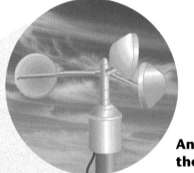

An anemometer gives the speed of a wind.

Wind speed is measured with a device called an anemometer (an′ə mom′i tər). An anemometer is a series of cups mounted on a shaft that can spin freely. When the wind blows against the cups, they spin like a pinwheel. The faster the wind blows, the faster the cups spin the shaft. A speedometer is attached to the shaft and calibrated to measure wind speed. Can you pick out the anemometer in the array of instruments at this weather station?

What Is the Beaufort Scale?

In 1805 Sir Francis Beaufort of the British Navy devised a system for measuring wind speed by observing its effect on the surface of the sea. He assigned a number from 0 to 12 to each effect. This is the Beaufort scale.

Wind can be very useful. It is often used as a source of power. Winds turn special machinery—windmills—that produce electricity. It runs the machinery that grinds grain. It is still used today to pump water.

Wind also carries pollen to flowers. Seeds form as a result. Many kinds of seeds, in turn, are carried by wind to new places.

BEAUFORT WIND SCALE

Type of Wind	Kilometers per Hour	Miles per Hour	Observations
0 Calm	less than 1	less than 0.6	Calm; smoke rises straight up
1 Light air	1–5	0.6–3	Weather vanes don't move
2 Light breeze	6–11	4–7	Weather vanes move slightly
3 Gentle breeze	12–19	8–12	Leaves move; flags stretch out
4 Moderate breeze	20–29	13–18	Small branches sway
5 Fresh breeze	30–38	19–24	Trees sway; white caps on ponds
6 Strong breeze	39–50	25–31	Large branches sway
7 Moderate gale	51–61	32–38	Hard to walk into the wind
8 Fresh gale	62–74	39–46	Branches break off trees
9 Strong gale	75–87	47–54	Shingles blow off roofs
10 Whole gale	88–101	55–63	Trees are uprooted
11 Storm	102–117	64–73	Extensive damage
12 Hurricane	118+	74+	Violent destruction

REVIEW

1. What makes air pressure change?

2. What causes wind to blow in a particular direction?

3. Why are there zones of winds around the world?

4. USE NUMBERS/INTERPRET DATA On a weather map, how can you compare the speed and direction of winds?

5. CRITICAL THINKING *Apply* How might you make a simple device to tell wind direction?

WHY IT MATTERS THINK ABOUT IT
How would you use simple observation to get an idea of how fast the wind is moving?

WHY IT MATTERS WRITE ABOUT IT
What are some ways people can actually make use of the wind?

READING SKILL
Write a paragraph describing the main idea and supporting details of this lesson.

In Tune with the Monsoon

Who's in tune with the monsoon winds? Nearly half of Earth's population! The word *monsoon* is Arabic for "season." Aptly named, monsoons change direction with the seasons. Winds blow in one direction for about six months, then in the opposite direction for about six months.

We often hear about monsoons in India and Pakistan, but did you know that other places also have them? Places include Africa, South America, Australia, and even the southern United States!

Why do monsoons change direction? In summer the Sun heats dry air over tropical land, while nearby oceans stay cooler. The warm air rises above the land, and cooler air from the ocean blows in to take its place. The wind blowing from the ocean brings heavy rain from June to October.

In winter the land cools off. Then as warm air rises over the ocean, cool air from the land rushes in to take its place. From November until May, a dry wind blows from the land out to the ocean.

Summer winds

Winter winds

Geography Link

In one part of India, the average winter rainfall is 2.54 centimeters (1 inch) a month. During the summer it gets up to 2.54 meters (100 inches) of rain a month!

Farmers depend on the monsoons. When the rain starts, farmers plant rice and other crops. If monsoons come late, nothing grows on the dusty land. However, really heavy rains can wash away the crops!

In 1998 monsoons killed more than 1,000 people in India and Bangladesh and left millions homeless.

DISCUSSION STARTER

How do you think the monsoons affect people in monsoon regions who aren't farmers?

To learn more about the monsoons, visit *www.mhschool.com/science* and enter the keyword MONSOON.

*inter*NET
CONNECTION

SCIENCE WORDS

air pressure p.105   evaporation p.112

cirrus cloud p.122   humidity p.112

condensation p.113   precipitation p.124

Coriolis effect p.138   stratus cloud p.122

cumulus cloud p.122   water vapor p.112

USING SCIENCE WORDS

Number a paper from 1 to 10. Fill in 1 to 5 with words from the list above.

1. Rain, snow, and sleet are kinds of ___?___.

2. The ___?___ causes winds to follow a curved path over Earth's surface.

3. A(n) ___?___ forms in blanketlike layers.

4. Liquid changes directly to a gas by the process called ___?___.

5. The amount of water vapor in the air is called ___?___.

6–10. Pick five words from the list above that were not used in 1 to 5, and use each in a sentence.

UNDERSTANDING SCIENCE IDEAS

11. Describe three kinds of clouds.

12. Where does weather take place?

13. How do water droplets form on the outside of a cold glass on a warm, humid day?

14. What are isobars?

15. What determines the amount of sunlight a region gets during the summer?

USING IDEAS AND SKILLS

16. **READING SKILL: MAIN IDEA AND SUPPORTING DETAILS** Explain why north winds blow to the southwest.

17. Explain why hot days when the relative humidity is high are more uncomfortable than hot days when the relative humidity is low.

18. Why must both evaporation and condensation occur to have rain?

19. **USE NUMBERS/INTERPRET DATA** What kind of weather is city A having? City B?

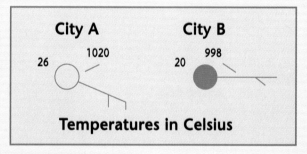

City A   City B

26   1020   20   998

Temperatures in Celsius

20. **THINKING LIKE A SCIENTIST** What if there were no plants? Do you think Earth would still get as much rain as it does now? State and explain a hypothesis. Describe how you might test your ideas.

PROBLEMS and PUZZLES

Draft Drift Observe updrafts and downdrafts in your classroom. Make a sketch of the room. Use a compass to determine north, south, east, and west. Drop a feather, and watch its drift. Mark the "wind direction" on your map. Repeat in many parts of the room. Explain your results.

CHAPTER 4
WEATHER PATTERNS AND CLIMATE

Changes in the weather help scientists predict the weather. They can help you plan activities over a few days.

You may also plan activities over a year. When does your area have the highest temperatures? The lowest? Do you get tornadoes? Hurricanes? Heavy rainfall? When? Temperatures and rainfall are part of a weather pattern in an area that repeats year after year.

In Chapter 4 you'll learn about how weather is predicted. You learn more about patterns that repeat each year.

In Chapter 4 you will read for sequence of events. You will read the events that lead up to a thunderstorm and tornado.

Topic
EARTH SCIENCE
5

WHY IT MATTERS

By studying air masses and fronts, we can predict changes in the weather.

SCIENCE WORDS

air mass a large region of the atmosphere where the air has similar properties throughout

front a boundary between air masses with different temperatures

cold front a boundary where cold air moves in under a mass of warm air

warm front a boundary where warm air moves in over a mass of cold air

occluded front a front formed where a cold front moves in under a warm front

stationary front an unmoving front where a cold air mass and a warm air mass meet

Air Masses and Fronts

Should you plan a trip to the beach tomorrow? Or would it be wiser to locate your umbrella? The answer depends on knowing what kind of weather is on the way. To predict this, both you and weather forecasters can turn to weather maps. The maps show conditions at different weather stations across the country. They also show how weather is changing. This map is a simple kind of weather map you might see in a newspaper.

EXPLORE

HYPOTHESIZE How can you tell where the weather may change? Write a hypothesis in your *Science Journal*. Test your ideas. How would you use a weather map to give a weather report of the country?

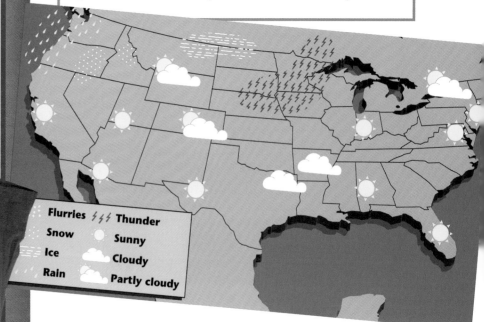

Flurries	⚡⚡	Thunder	
Snow	○	Sunny	
Ice		Cloudy	
Rain		Partly cloudy	

EXPLORE ACTIVITY

Investigate How to Compare Weather

Use a map and key to predict the weather.

PROCEDURES

COMMUNICATE Think of the country in large regions—the Northeast, the Southwest, and so on. Think of regions like the Pacific Coast, the Atlantic Coast, and the Gulf Coast. In your *Science Journal,* write a report for the weather in each region based on the map you see here.

CONCLUDE AND APPLY

1. INFER Which areas are having warm, rainy weather?

2. INFER Where is the weather cool and dry?

GOING FURTHER: Problem Solving

3. INFER How do you think weather in any part of the country may change, based on the data in this map? Give reasons for your answer. How would you check your predictions?

4. INTERPRET DATA Using weather maps in a newspaper, or the one on page 148, describe the weather.

MATERIALS
- station model key
- newspaper weather map (optional)
- pencil
- crayons
- newspaper
- *Science Journal*

W   E

San Francisco

Lines are drawn to show wind direction, not speed. This is a wind coming from the east, going west—an eastwind.

CANADA

55 1014 Seattle
47 1020 Butte
30 1013 Bismark
Minneapolis 34 1010
Buffalo 40 1008
Boston 39 1014
Detroit 44® 1039
42® 1011 New York
Chicago 40 1004
Cincinatti 60® 1001
Richmond 45® 1008
57 1025 Salt Lake City
60 1014 San Francisco
51 1020 Denver
Kansas City 50 1011
62 1015 Los Angeles
68 1017 Phoenix
54 1013 Oklahoma City
71 1009 Atlanta
57 1016 Roswell
58 1014 Fort Worth
Jacksonville 72 1016
60® 1011 76® 1010 New Orleans
Galveston
Miami 80 1020
®=rain

MEXICO

N
NW NE
W   E
SW SE
S

Temperatures here are given in Fahrenheit degrees.

149

AIR MASSES

Continental
polar (cP)
cold, dry air

Maritime
polar (mP)
cool, moist air

Maritime
polar (mP)
cool, moist air

Pacific
Ocean

Atlantic
Ocean

Maritime
tropical (mT)
warm, moist air

Continental
tropical (cT)
hot, dry air

Maritime
tropical (mT)
warm, moist air

How Can We Compare Weather?

The Explore Activity showed that cities across a large region can share the same weather. It also showed how the weather in different areas can differ.

Why are weather conditions in one part of a country different from those in another part? Look back at the map on page 149. Some of the cities are having clear, cool weather. The air throughout this region is cool and dry.

Other cities are having warmer, cloudy weather. The air throughout this region is warm and moist. A large

region of the atmosphere where the air has similar properties throughout is called an air mass.

An air mass gets its properties from the region where it forms. Air over the Gulf of Mexico is above very warm water. The water warms the air, and evaporation from the Gulf adds water vapor. The air becomes warm and moist. Air masses are named for the region they come from.

As air masses move, they bring these conditions with them. What happens if a cool, moist air mass moves over an area that has warm, dry weather? The warm, dry weather will change.

Once an air mass is formed, it is moved by global winds. In the United States, global winds tend to move air masses from west to east.

Air masses with different conditions can "meet." That is, one runs into another. What happens when air masses with different temperatures meet? They don't mix together. Instead, a narrow boundary forms between them. This boundary is called a front. It marks the leading edge, or front, of an air mass that is moving into an area where another air mass is moving out. Weather changes rapidly at fronts. That's because you pass from one kind of air mass into another. Fronts often cause rainy, unsettled weather. There are several types of fronts that can form.

Brain Power

When air masses meet, they form fronts. What do you think happens when two fronts meet?

A WEATHER FRONT

A front forms along the boundary between a warm air mass and a cold air mass.

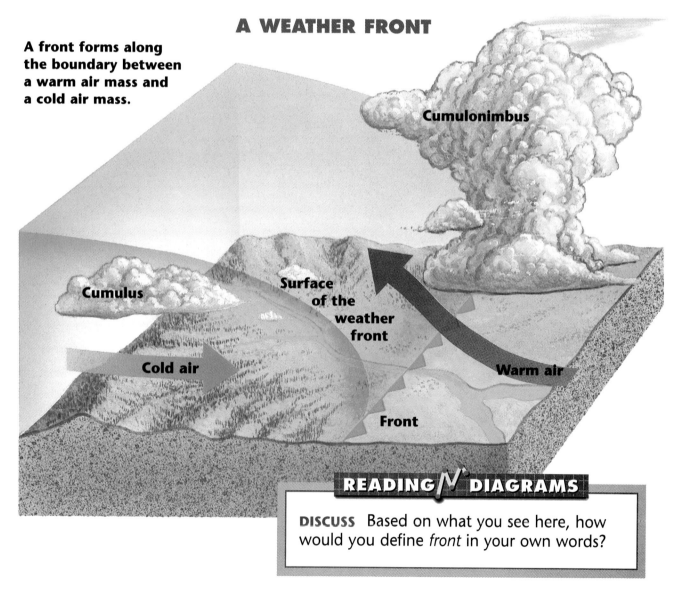

Cumulonimbus

Cumulus

Surface of the weather front

Cold air

Warm air

Front

READING DIAGRAMS

DISCUSS Based on what you see here, how would you define *front* in your own words?

151

What Kinds of Fronts Are There?

There are several kinds of fronts. How do fronts make the weather change?

- In a **cold front**, cold air moves in under a warm air mass. Cold fronts often bring brief, heavy storms. There may be thunderstorms and strong winds. After the storm the skies are usually clearer, and the weather is usually cooler and drier.

- In a **warm front**, warm air moves in over a cold air mass. Warm fronts often bring light, steady rain or snow. The precipitation may last for days. Winds are usually light. Warm fronts may also bring fog—stratus clouds that form near the ground. Afterward the weather is usually warmer and more humid.

- An **occluded** (ə klüd′əd) **front** occurs when a cold front and a warm front meet. A fast-moving cold front

WEATHER PRODUCED BY FRONTS

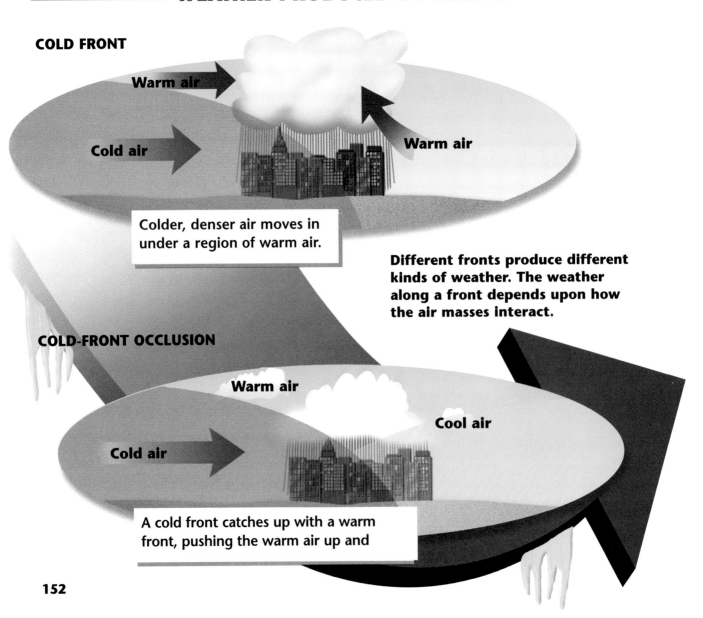

COLD FRONT

Warm air

Cold air

Warm air

Colder, denser air moves in under a region of warm air.

Different fronts produce different kinds of weather. The weather along a front depends upon how the air masses interact.

COLD-FRONT OCCLUSION

Warm air

Cool air

Cold air

A cold front catches up with a warm front, pushing the warm air up and moves in on a warm front. There are two ways this can happen:

In a cold-front occlusion, the air behind the front is cold. The air ahead of the warm front is cool. What is happening is that cold air is moving in on cool air and warm air is pushed up between them. The weather along this front will be like that produced by a cold front.

In a warm-front occlusion, the air behind the incoming cold front is just cool, not cold. The air in front of the warm front, however, might be cold. Then the weather will be more like that produced by a warm front.

• A cold air mass and a warm air mass may meet and remain over an area for days without moving. This is called a **stationary front**. Stationary fronts usually have calm weather.

READING ⁄ DIAGRAMS

1. **WRITE** Write a paragraph comparing a warm front with a cold front.
2. **DISCUSS** Write an explanation of what an occluded front is.

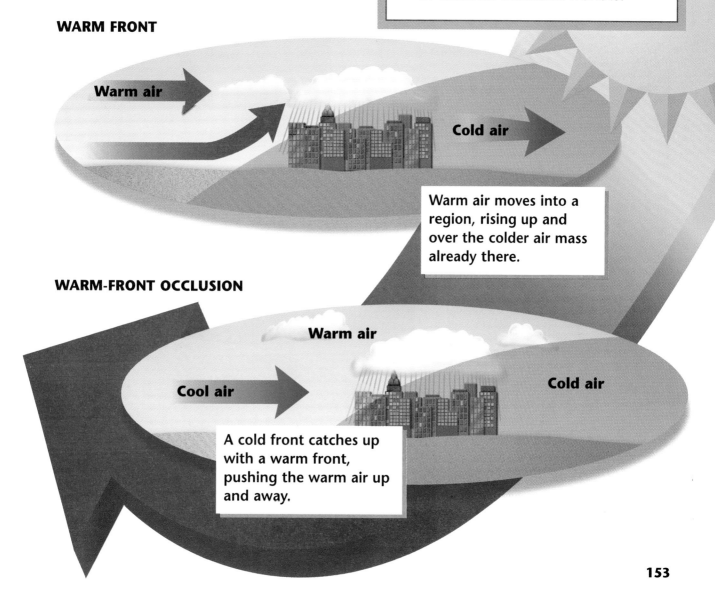

WARM FRONT

Warm air

Cold air

Warm air moves into a region, rising up and over the colder air mass already there.

WARM-FRONT OCCLUSION

Warm air

Cool air

Cold air

A cold front catches up with a warm front, pushing the warm air up and away.

What Do Fronts Look Like from Space?

Pictures taken from space are great tools for seeing large weather patterns, such as fronts and storms. Scientists send up satellites in orbit around Earth. Some of these satellites are equipped to take pictures of weather patterns. These satellites move in orbit in a way that allows them to follow a weather pattern as it moves slowly across Earth's surface.

To find fronts on a satellite map, look for swirling lines of clouds. The curved lines often mark the movement of fronts.

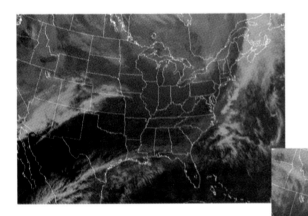

Weather satellites are located above the equator. They are more than 36,000 km (20,000 miles) above Earth's surface. Several of these satellites work together to produce a nearly complete picture of the globe every half-hour.

Why Are Fronts Important?

Fronts are an important clue to how weather will change. As a front moves, areas just ahead of the front are about to have a change in weather. The weather may be cool and dry before a front approaches. The weather then becomes rainy and hot as the front passes by.

When fronts collide, scientists can locate places where the weather may change quickly, even dangerously. Sudden storms may break out. Knowing about fronts helps scientists to stay on the alert!

READING MAPS

1. **DISCUSS** Where do you see low pressure systems in the satellite picture? What do the clouds appear to be doing?
2. **WRITE** What kind of weather is happening in different parts of the country in each map? Explain.

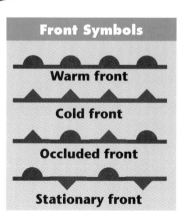

Front Symbols
Warm front
Cold front
Occluded front
Stationary front

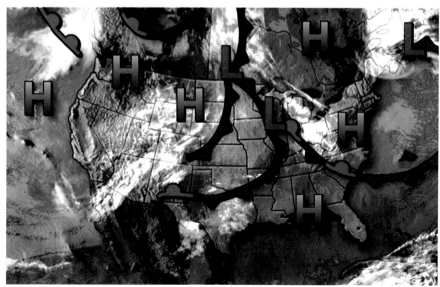

QUICK LAB

Weather Prediction

HYPOTHESIZE How can you use a weather map to predict the weather? Write a hypothesis in your *Science Journal*.

MATERIALS
• *Science Journal*

PROCEDURES

1. **ANALYZE** The map shows weather in the United States at 6 P.M. on October 29. In your *Science Journal*, describe the weather in Washington, D.C. The temperatures are in degrees Celsius.

2. **ANALYZE** In your *Science Journal*, describe the weather in the northwest part of the country and the southeast.

CONCLUDE AND APPLY

INFER Weather patterns move from west to east across the United States. How do you think the weather in Washington, D.C., will change in the next day or so? Explain your answer.

How Is Weather Forecasting Done?

Scientists usually forecast the weather using a *synoptic weather map*. This type of map shows a summary of the weather using station models. By comparing maps made every six hours, scientists can tell how weather systems are moving. They then use this information to predict what the weather will be like hours later.

If you look at weather records to see what happened in the past, you can find patterns. *Statistical forecasting* is based on finding patterns.

For example, suppose you notice that the wind has just started blowing from the west. Past records show that 75 out of the last 100 times the wind blew from the west, your weather became clearer and colder. What weather prediction would you make?

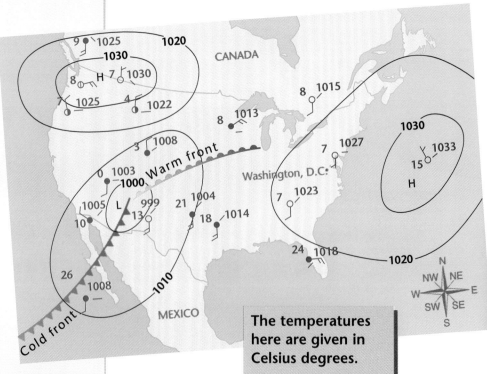

The temperatures here are given in Celsius degrees.

How Else Is Forecasting Done?

Spaceships going to the Moon aren't aimed directly at the Moon. The Moon is always moving. The spaceship aims at where the Moon will be when the ship arrives. Scientists use the spaceship's speed and direction to calculate where this spot is. In the same way, knowing how the atmosphere is moving lets you predict the weather.

The problem is that the atmosphere is huge and complex. Even simple predictions require millions of calculations. This couldn't be done without computers. Computers do high-speed calculations to predict the atmosphere's motion. Predictions are compared with forecasts to account for any differences. Two-day forecasts are calculated every 12 hours. A five-day forecast is calculated daily.

No one can be sure about how the weather will change. A weather forecaster might give a clear prediction of tomorrow's weather. However, another air mass might move in. Everything can change.

Still many people and industries rely on accurate forecasts. Farmers need to know if heavy rains or frosts are coming. Ski slopes must be aware of how much snow is expected. Vacationers use forecasts to plan trips.

REVIEW

1. What are four different kinds of air masses? How are they different?

2. **CAUSE AND EFFECT** What kind of weather is produced by a cold front? A warm front?

3. How can satellites help predict the weather?

4. How can weather maps help predict the weather?

5. **CRITICAL THINKING** *Apply* How can you tell what kind of front is passing by just by observing the weather?

WHY IT MATTERS THINK ABOUT IT
Why do you think people listen to the weather report?

WHY IT MATTERS WRITE ABOUT IT
How can changes in the weather affect how you spend your day?

Weather Watch: Then and Now

The barometer is invented. Changes in air pressure help modern scientists predict the weather.

The telegraph is invented. Forecasters begin talking to one another and sharing information.

400 B.C.   A.D. 1643   1732   1840   1870

Aristotle writes one of the first books about weather. He tries to explain rain, snow, and other "meteors" from the sky!

Benjamin Franklin writes *Poor Richard's Almanac,* in which he predicts the next year's weather. He bases his forecasts on what he sees and a few measurements.

A telegraph system is set up across the nation. The system is used to collect weather data and warn people about storms.

Poor Richard, 1733.

AN

Almanack

For the Year of Chrift

1733,

Being the Firft after LEAP YEAR.

And makes fince the Creation Years
By the Account of the Eaftern Greeks   7241
By the Latin Church, when ☉ ent. ♈   6932
By the Computation of W.W.   5742
By the Roman Chronology   5682
By the Jewifh Rabbies.   3494

History of Science

Four scientists in Norway use math and physics to explain weather and identify weather patterns.

Doppler radar is developed. It compares radio waves sent out with those that bounce back. The greater the difference, the faster a storm is moving.

Two kinds of satellites track weather patterns. One orbits about 36,000 kilometers (22,000 miles) above Earth, monitoring changes in storm systems. The other orbits only 850 kilometers (530 miles) above Earth to provide details about cloud systems.

| 1918 | 1940 | 1954 | 1960 | Today |

During World War II, radar is used to locate storms by bouncing radio waves off raindrops in clouds.

NASA sends up its first weather satellite.

DISCUSSION STARTER

How do you think computers have helped make weather predictions more accurate?

To learn more about weather watching, visit *www.mhschool.com/science* and enter the keyword WATCH.

*inter*NET
CONNECTION

Topic 6
EARTH SCIENCE

WHY IT MATTERS

Knowing about severe storms can save lives.

SCIENCE WORDS

thunderstorm the most common severe storm, formed in cumulonimbus clouds

tornado a violent whirling wind that moves across the ground in a narrow path

hurricane a very large, swirling storm with very low pressure at the center

storm surge a great rise of the sea along a shore caused by low pressure

Severe Storms

What's it like to be in the path of a tornado? People have reported a sound like the rumble of an approaching freight train. A tornado packs a windy wallop far more powerful than any train, however. Tornadoes are the most powerful storms on Earth. Although most tornadoes are not very wide and they don't last too long, when they touch down *watch out!* Like deadly whirling brooms, they can sweep away anything in their paths.

EXPLORE

HYPOTHESIZE Tornadoes strike all parts of the United States. However, they are more frequent in some regions than in others. Where in the U.S. is "tornado country"? Write a hypothesis in your *Science Journal*. How might you test your hypothesis?

160

Investigate What Severe Storms Are

To investigate what severe storms are, begin by plotting tornadoes on a map to tell where they are most likely to happen.

PROCEDURES

1. INFER The table shown here lists how many tornadoes occurred in each state over a 30-year period. It also shows about how many tornadoes occur in each state each year. Look at the data in the table for two minutes. Now write in your *Science Journal* what part of the country you think gets the most tornadoes.

2. COLLECT DATA Use the red marker to record the number of tornadoes that occurred in each state over the 30-year period. Use the blue marker to record the average number of tornadoes that occurred in a year in each state.

CONCLUDE AND APPLY

1. USE NUMBERS Which states had fewer than 10 tornadoes a year? Which states had more than 20 tornadoes a year?

2. INTERPRET DATA Which six states had the most tornadoes during the 30-year period?

3. INTERPRET DATA Which part of the country had the most tornadoes?

GOING FURTHER: Problem Solving

4. DRAW CONCLUSIONS Many people refer to a certain part of the country as "Tornado Alley." Which part of the country do you think that is? Why do you think people call it that? What else might these states have in common? Describe how you would go about finding the answer to that question.

MATERIALS

- map of U.S., including Alaska and Hawaii
- blue marker
- red marker
- *Science Journal*

State	Total	Average per year
AL	668	22
AK	0	0
AZ	106	4
AR	596	20
CA	148	5
CO	781	26
CT	37	1
DE	31	1
FL	1,590	53
GA	615	21
HI	25	1
ID	80	3
IL	798	27
IN	604	20
IA	1,079	36
KS	1,198	40
KY	296	10
LA	831	28
ME	50	2
MD	86	3
MA	89	3
MI	567	19
MN	607	20
MS	775	26
MO	781	26
MT	175	6
NE	1,118	37
NV	41	1
NH	56	2
NJ	78	3
NM	276	9
NY	169	6
NC	435	15
ND	621	21
OH	463	15
OK	1,412	47
OR	34	1
PA	310	10
RI	7	0
SC	307	10
SD	864	29
TN	360	12
TX	4,174	139
UT	58	2
VT	21	1
VA	188	6
WA	45	2
WV	69	2
WI	625	21
WY	356	12

What Are Severe Storms?

The Explore Activity was about a violent kind of storm. It does not happen all the time. It forms under special conditions. Often this storm grows out of another, more common kind of storm—a **thunderstorm**.

Thunderstorms are the most common kind of severe storm. They form in clouds called *thunderheads*—cumulonimbus clouds. The storms cause huge electric sparks called *lightning*. The lightning heats the air and causes the noise called *thunder*. Thunderstorms usually have heavy rains and strong winds. Some thunderstorms also produce hail.

First Stage

A thunderstorm starts when intense heating causes air to rise very quickly. A cloud forms where there is an upward rush of heated air, an *updraft*. As more and more warm, moist air is carried upward, the cloud grows larger and larger. Strong updrafts keep droplets of water and ice crystals in the cloud, so they grow in size, too. When the updrafts can't support them anymore, they fall as heavy rain or even hail. Look at the downpour falling from this thunderstorm.

Second Stage

Once the rain falls, it causes downdrafts in the cloud. That is, air moves downward. When the air going up rubs against air going down, static electricity builds up. When enough builds up, there's a huge spark—lightning.

Lightning is unpredictable. It may jump from the cloud to the ground or from the ground to the cloud. It may jump between two thunderclouds. It may also jump from one spot to

HOW A THUNDERSTORM FORMS

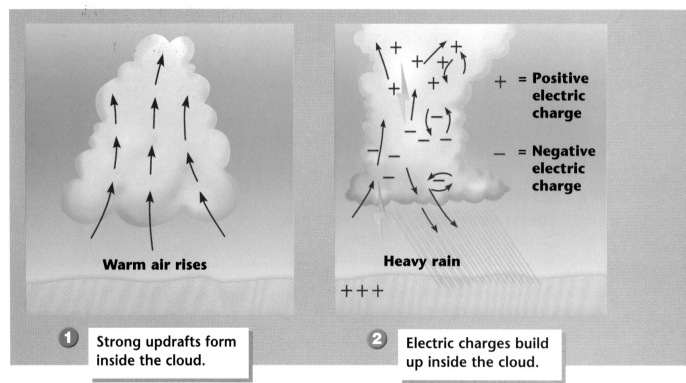

Warm air rises

Heavy rain

+ = Positive electric charge

− = Negative electric charge

+++

1 Strong updrafts form inside the cloud.

2 Electric charges build up inside the cloud.

Brain Power

In some parts of the country, people worry more about thunderstorms than they do in other regions. Why do you think this is so?

another within the cloud. Lightning superheats the air so the air suddenly expands. It slams into the air around it with such force that it makes a mighty sound—thunder.

Third Stage

The storm dies when a downdraft becomes stronger than the updraft. Heavy rain lightens up and stops.

Thunderstorms usually form in the warm air just ahead of a cold front. The cold, dense air wedges under the warm, moist air and causes the warm air to rise rapidly. Be on the lookout for thunderstorms. They are likely when the weather is hot and humid and a cold front is approaching.

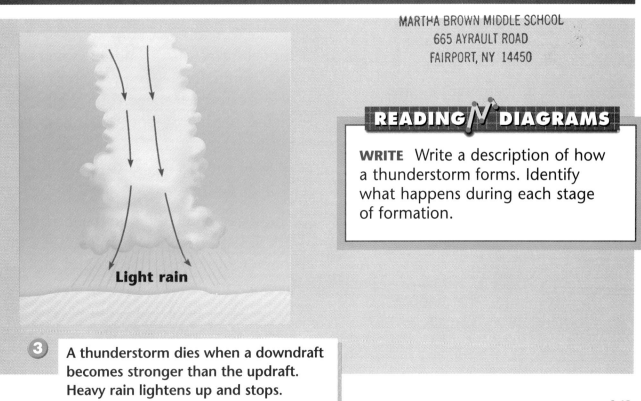

Light rain

MARTHA BROWN MIDDLE SCHOOL
665 AYRAULT ROAD
FAIRPORT, NY 14450

READING IN DIAGRAMS

WRITE Write a description of how a thunderstorm forms. Identify what happens during each stage of formation.

3 A thunderstorm dies when a downdraft becomes stronger than the updraft. Heavy rain lightens up and stops.

QUICK LAB

Tornado in a Bottle

HYPOTHESIZE How does a tornado form? Write a hypothesis in your *Science Journal*.

MATERIALS
- two 2-L plastic bottles
- duct tape
- water
- paper towel
- pencil
- *Science Journal*

PROCEDURES

1. MAKE A MODEL Fill one bottle one-third full of water. Dry the neck of the bottle, and tape over the top. Use the pencil to poke a hole in the tape.

2. Place the other bottle upside down over the mouth of the first bottle. Tape the two bottles together.

3. OBSERVE Hold the bottles by the necks so the one with the water is on top. Swirl them around while your partner gently squeezes on the empty bottle. Then place the bottles on a desk with the water bottle on top. Describe in your *Science Journal* what you see.

CONCLUDE AND APPLY

INFER How is this like what happens when a tornado forms? Explain.

How and Where Do Tornadoes Happen?

The most violent thunderstorms often spin off even more dangerous storms—tornadoes. A tornado is a violent whirling wind that moves across the ground in a narrow path.

How They Happen

Late in the day, when Earth's surface is very warm, convection can get very strong. This can lead to a tornado. A tornado is sort of a runaway convection cell.

- When the updraft in a convection cell is really strong, the air rushes in from all sides at high speeds.

- The air curves into a spin. This lowers the pressure even more. Air rushes in even faster, and the pressure gets even lower, and so on. Like a spinning skater who pulls her arms in close to her sides, the spinning tornado gets faster and faster.

- As the tornado gets stronger, a funnel forms that eventually touches the ground. In the center of a tornado, winds can reach speeds of 500 kilometers per hour (about 300 miles per hour) or more. At such high speeds, winds can destroy anything in their path.

The speed of the wind in the tornado is not the speed with which the tornado moves across the ground. It moves across the ground very fast but can change its direction continually.

Where They Happen

As the Explore Activity shows, most tornadoes in the United States seem to occur in the Midwest and in the South.

Tornadoes form where dry, cold air masses mix with warm, moist air masses. In the United States, this is most likely to happen in the Great Plains region and the Mississippi Valley. Florida also gets lots of tornadoes.

Tornadoes are most likely to occur when there are big differences in the air masses. This happens most often in early spring and summer. Tornadoes can also form over water. Such tornadoes are called *waterspouts.*

More tornadoes occur in the United States than in any other country, especially in the area known as Tornado Alley.

Tornado Alley

READING ∿ MAPS

WRITE What states are included in Tornado Alley?

A tornado has a characteristic funnel-shaped cloud.

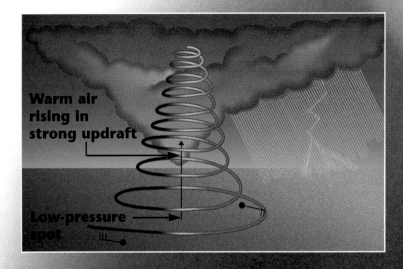

Warm air rising in strong updraft

Low-pressure spot

READING ∿ DIAGRAMS

1. DISCUSS Where is the pressure lowest in the tornado?

2. DISCUSS In what direction is the wind spinning—clockwise (like the hands of a clock) or counter-clockwise (the opposite)?

How Do Hurricanes Form?

If you live near an ocean or the Gulf Coast, you may have experienced a **hurricane**. Hurricanes are very large, swirling storms with very low pressure at their center. They form over tropical oceans—near the equator.

Air masses near the equator tend to be very much alike. They don't form the fronts that you learned about in Topic 5. Instead, they form lots of thunderstorms.

- As global winds push these thunderstorms along, they line up in rows. Strong heating and lots of evaporation over the ocean can cause a large low-pressure center to form. If this happens winds begin to blow in toward the low.

- The Coriolis effect causes winds to spiral counterclockwise in the Northern Hemisphere. Clusters of thunderstorms are pulled into the spiral. The thunderstorms merge, forming a single large storm.

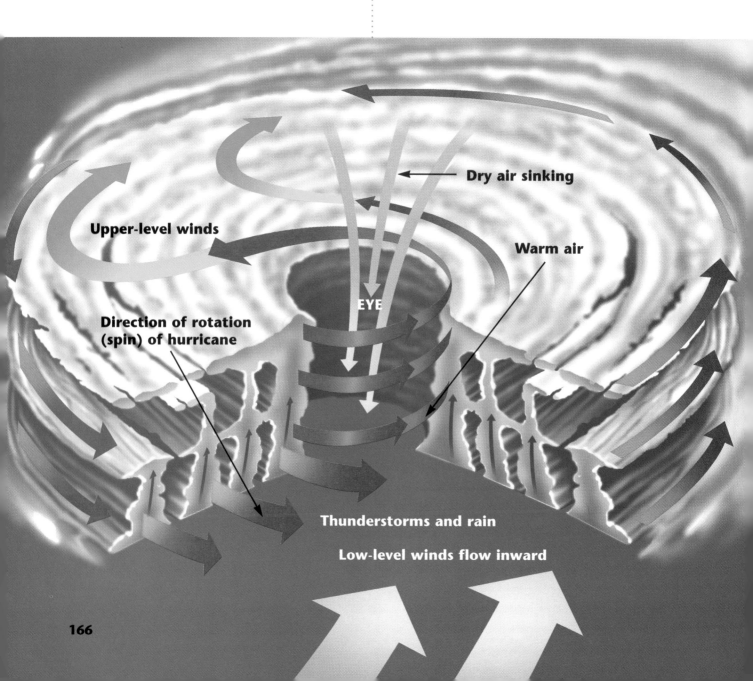

Dry air sinking

Upper-level winds

Warm air

EYE

Direction of rotation (spin) of hurricane

Thunderstorms and rain

Low-level winds flow inward

- As water vapor in the storms condenses, heat is released. The air is warmed. This decreases the air's density and pressure. Moisture evaporating into the air decreases the air's density and pressure even more. Low air pressure favors more evaporation. This lowers the pressure even more.

- The lower the air pressure, the faster are the winds that blow in toward the center of the storm. When the winds reach speeds of 120 kilometers per hour (about 75 miles per hour) or higher, the storm is a hurricane.

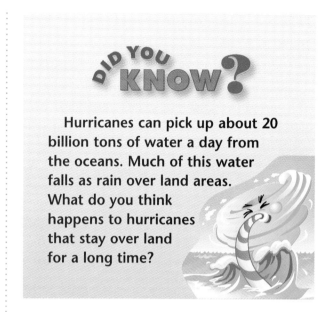

DID YOU KNOW?

Hurricanes can pick up about 20 billion tons of water a day from the oceans. Much of this water falls as rain over land areas. What do you think happens to hurricanes that stay over land for a long time?

- As the moist air in the storm rises and cools, condensation takes place. The clouds thicken. Heavy rains fall through the high winds. When fully formed a hurricane has an eye at its center. The eye is an area of light winds and skies that are nearly clear.

Hurricanes can easily grow to more than 700 kilometers (about 400 miles) in diameter. As you can see from the drawing, the image of Hurricane Fran shows it to be almost as large as the entire state of Florida!

Satellite photograph of a hurricane and its eye

Direction of wind

Eye

READING *N* DIAGRAMS

1. **DISCUSS** In which direction do winds turn in a hurricane—clockwise (the direction of the hands of a clock) or counter clockwise (the opposite)?
2. **DISCUSS** Where is the pressure the lowest?
3. **DISCUSS** Where is rain happening?

How Do Hurricanes Affect Ocean Waves?

Just north of the equator, gentle global winds move hurricanes west to northwest at 10 to 20 kilometers per hour (6 to 12 miles per hour). As they move north, away from the equator, their speed tends to increase.

Hurricane winds whip up large waves in the ocean. These waves move outward from the storm and pound against a shore for days before the storm arrives. However, it is the storm surge that causes the most destruction. Storm surge is a great rise of the sea along a shore. Its main cause is low air pressure!

Air pressure normally presses down on the surface of the sea like a giant hand. When the pressure drops in a hurricane, it is like lifting the hand slightly. The surface of the sea rises, forming a bulge beneath a hurricane.

When the hurricane moves over a coast, the bulge can cause water levels to suddenly rise several feet, or surge.

Hurricane winds also push water ahead of the storm, forcing water onshore and adding to the storm surge. If the storm surge comes at high tide, it is even worse. Great storms have surges that raise the water level by 7 meters (about 20 feet) or more.

During a great storm, the surge, large waves, high winds, and torrential rain of the storm all happen at the same time. Low-lying coastal areas are flooded. Beachfront homes are destroyed. Beaches can get worn away.

A Real Hurricane—Fran

On August 22, 1996, a storm formed off the coast of Africa and began moving west-northwest at about 10 miles per hour. By August 29 it had become more concentrated. Winds reached hurricane strength. Hurricane Fran was born. Fran continued moving west and was even stronger by the time it skirted the Bahamas. By September 5, 1996, Fran had 105-knot winds and was 400 km (250 miles) off the Florida coast.

A large low-pressure system over Tennessee steered it westward, and it struck North Carolina and Virginia on September 6. Winds of 120 knots were clocked off Cape Fear as Fran came ashore. Sea level surged to 3.6 m (12 feet) above normal. As much as 40 cm (12 inches) of rain fell in parts of North Carolina. Thirty-four people died. Flash flooding caused most deaths. A storm surge on the North Carolina coast destroyed many beachfront houses.

High winds damaged trees and roofs. They also downed power lines, leaving 4.5 million people without power. Nearly half a million people were ordered to evacuate the coast. Altogether it is estimated that Fran caused 3.2 billion dollars of damage.

Hurricanes begin to die out when they move over land. Cut off from the warm ocean, the hurricane has no water to replace what falls as rain. Friction between the winds and the land decreases wind speed. When it has been over land long enough, it will completely die out.

Once Hurricane Fran moved ashore, it steadily weakened. By the time it reached central North Carolina, it was no longer a hurricane. By the time it reached the Great Lakes on September 9, it was no longer even a storm. The remains of Fran disappeared on September 10.

READING / MAPS

1. **WRITE** What ocean does a hurricane have to cross as it approaches North America from Africa?
2. **WRITE** What part of North America did Hurricane Fran reach?

GEOGRAPHY LINK

North America

Atlantic Ocean

Bahamas

Africa

South America

Severe storms can cause damage.

What Can You Do to Be Safe in a Storm?

Hurricanes, tornadoes, and thunderstorms can be very dangerous. In order to stay safe in these storms, you need to follow certain safety rules.

IF YOU HEAR STORM WATCHES OR WARNINGS ON TV OR RADIO, FOLLOW THEIR DIRECTIONS CAREFULLY!

A storm watch means that conditions are right for a storm to form. A storm warning means that a storm has been spotted and is heading your way.

Thunderstorm Safety Rules

1. Go inside a house or large building, but don't go into a small building that stands off by itself. It is also safe to stay inside a closed car or truck (not a convertible!). Be sure the doors and windows are closed. Do not touch any metal inside the car.

2. Stay away from pipes, faucets, electrical outlets, and open windows.

3. Don't use the telephone, except in an emergency. Electricity can travel through phone lines.

4. Stay away from the water. If you are in the water, GET OUT. Do not go out in a boat. Lightning is attracted to water.

5. If you are outside, be sure you are not the tallest thing around. Be sure, also, that you are not standing near or under the tallest thing around. Do not stand up on a beach, in an open field, or on a hilltop. Do not stand under a tree. Do not stand under an object that is standing alone in an open area.

6. If you are stuck in an open area, crouch down. Stay away from metal objects, including bicycles, motorcycles, farm equipment, golf clubs, and golf carts.

7. If your hair feels like it's standing on end, lightning may be about to strike. Crouch down. Lean forward, and put your hands on your knees. Try to make yourself as low to the ground as possible while touching as little of the ground as you can.

Tornado Safety Rules

The National Weather Service issues a tornado watch when conditions for a tornado exist. Be on the alert. If a tornado is spotted, a tornado warning is given. Take action immediately.

1. At home open the windows slightly, then seek shelter. Stay away from windows and doors.

2. The safest place is in a storm cellar. The next safest is a basement. Stay under a table, staircase, or mattress. If you have no storm cellar or basement, seek shelter in a strong building. Stay on the ground floor. Stay under a table or bed, or in a closet.

3. Do not stay in a mobile home.

4. Outdoors lie facedown in a ditch. Cover your head to protect yourself from flying debris.

5. At school go to an inside hallway on the lowest floor. If your school has a tornado shelter, go there. Follow your teacher's or principal's directions.

Hurricane Safety Rules

1. People living in coastal areas may be warned to board up their homes and head for safer, inland areas. If you live in an area connected to the mainland by a bridge, be sure you allow plenty of time to leave. Traffic on the bridge may be very heavy. People who live in low-lying areas that flood in heavy rains may also be warned to go to shelters.

2. Board or tape up windows and glass doors. Bring outdoor objects—such as furniture, bikes, potted plants—indoors.

3. Be sure you stock up on bottled water, canned and packaged foods, and first-aid supplies and medicines for the family and pets. Don't forget flashlights and fresh batteries. Test the flashlights ahead of time to be sure the bulbs are working. You may be without power for several days. Be sure the food you have can be eaten without cooking.

4. If your home is on sturdy, high ground, stay there. Otherwise go to a shelter.

5. Don't be fooled by the eye of the hurricane. Everything may be calm. Skies may be fair for a short time, but the rest of the hurricane's fury is right behind the eye.

How Can We Find Storms?

Storms are hard to predict because they form so quickly. Scientists use the best methods possible to identify conditions before a storm "brews." They look for clues, like the movement of fronts and the formation of very low pressure areas. Once these conditions are located, scientists keep a "weather eye" on them to see how they develop.

Special methods are used to find storms as they form. One such method is Doppler radar. The word *radar* stands for *ra*dio *d*etection *a*nd *r*anging. Radar works by sending out radio waves and recording their echo. The change in the radio signal from the original to the echo tells us something about where it reflected.

Doppler radar looks at how the echoes have changed in frequency from the original signals. This information gives clues about the movement of the reflective surface. Doppler radar is a very good tool for scientists to track storms. The radio waves reflect off storm clouds and are picked back up again at the radar stations.

With Doppler radar scientists can tell if raindrops are moving toward or away from them. Doppler radar can also spot spinning motions of clouds. These motions help warn scientists that tornadoes or hurricanes may be forming. Scientists use Doppler radar to find and track thunderstorms, tornadoes, and hurricanes. Doppler radar helps forecasters predict which way the storms will travel.

Scientists have used radar systems to track storms since the 1950s. More recently they have begun to use NEXRAD. *NEXRAD* stands for *"NEX*t generation of weather *RAD*ar." NEXRAD is a new form of Doppler radar that is replacing older radar systems. NEXRAD can spot small particles such as blowing dust, very light snow, and even drizzle. NEXRAD is also more accurate than conventional radar at predicting floods and flash floods. It can show the exact locations of different fronts. It also shows changes in wind speed and direction. All of this information helps scientists make more and more accurate weather predictions.

Forecasters can warn people when dangerous storms are headed their way.

WHY IT MATTERS

The more you know about severe storms, the more you can be safe. The dangers of a thunderstorm can be avoided by following simple rules. When a thunderstorm approaches, think "safety first." Even if you are playing an important ball game, the game has to stop, and you have to take cover. Hurricanes may mean that you and your family may have to leave your home until the storm passes.

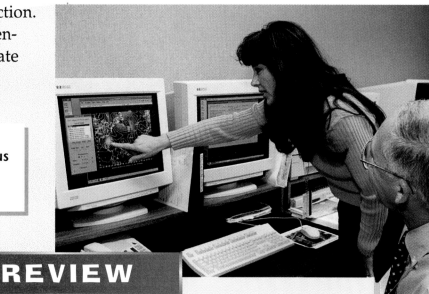

REVIEW

1. **SEQUENCE OF EVENTS** How does a thunderstorm form?

2. How is a tornado related to a thunderstorm?

3. What causes a hurricane to form? What moves it in a certain direction?

4. Why can hurricanes cause so much damage?

5. **CRITICAL THINKING** *Analyze* Why do you think predicting a severe storm is so difficult?

WHY IT MATTERS THINK ABOUT IT
What would you have to do to prepare for a severe storm that might hit your area?

WHY IT MATTERS WRITE ABOUT IT
What are the two or three most important rules for staying safe in a severe storm? Explain your answer.

READING SKILL

Write a paragraph to explain the sequence of events involved when a tornado forms.

SCIENCE MAGAZINE

Storm Tracking

It's easy for meteorologists to predict a storm that's part of a giant weather system; it's been reported by people experiencing it! Wind direction and changes in air pressure also signal a storm is near.

Smaller storm systems are harder to predict, but computers help. They are fed data about a storm's present location; current wind direction, air pressure, and rainfall; and how similar storms have behaved. The computer plots the path the storm will likely follow.

The use of radar has advanced hurricane prediction. Radar bounces radio waves off raindrops to discover where the storm is heading. Today, thanks to radar tracking, damage from hurricanes has been greatly reduced.

Tornadoes, or twisters, are the most violent windstorms. Because the right conditions for developing tornadoes occur quite often, they're hard to predict. The United States had more "killer tornadoes" during the first half of 1998 than in all of 1996 or 1997!

Doppler radar helps meteorologists predict tornadoes. It doesn't just spot a tornado's heavy rains, it tells the speed and direction of the funnel. With Doppler, people can be warned to seek cover before a twister hits!

There will be heavy rain all up the West Coast. Ships in the Pacific report storm conditions.

A tornado warning is in effect for Mills County. A tornado watch covers the rest of the region.

174

Science, Technology, and Society

DISCUSSION STARTER

1. How did people predict storms before the inventions of radio, computers, and radar?

2. Why does Doppler radar track storms better?

A large winter storm is in the North Atlantic. Computer projections show it will track inland and strike Boston early Friday, bringing gale winds and up to a foot of snow.

Hurricane Clyde is predicted to make landfall before dawn. People in coastal regions should secure their homes and head inland.

To learn more about tracking storms, visit *www.mhschool.com/science* and enter the keyword TRACKING.

*inter*NET
CONNECTION

Topic 7
EARTH SCIENCE

WHY IT MATTERS

All places on Earth have patterns of changes in weather that repeat over time.

SCIENCE WORDS

climate the average weather pattern of a region

radiative balance a balance between energy lost and energy gained

greenhouse effect the ability of the atmosphere to let in sunlight but to not let heat escape

Climate

What if you could live in each of these places? What would summers be like? What would winters be like? Which place do you think is wet and warm? Which is dry and cold? Which is hot and dry? Which place do you think has year-round weather most like yours? What evidence in the pictures did you use to answer these questions?

EXPLORE

HYPOTHESIZE What factors are used to describe the average weather pattern of a region? Write a hypothesis in your *Science Journal*. How might you use graphs of year-round weather in different places to test your ideas?

Investigate What Weather Patterns Tell You

Compare weather patterns in two cities.

MATERIALS
• *Science Journal*

PROCEDURES

1. USE NUMBERS Look at the graph for city 1. The bottom is labeled with the months of the year. The left side is labeled with the temperature in degrees Celsius. Use this scale to read the temperature line. What is the average temperature in city 1 during July?

2. USE NUMBERS The right side of the graph is labeled with millimeters of precipitation. Use this scale when reading the precipitation bars. What is the average precipitation in city 1 during July?

3. Repeat steps 1 and 2 for city 2.

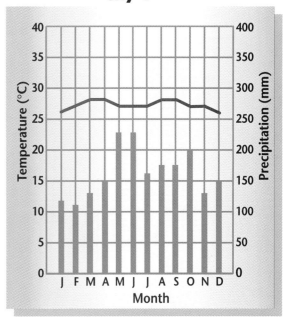

City 1

CONCLUDE AND APPLY

1. COMPARE AND CONTRAST How do the annual amounts of precipitation compare for the two cities? Record your answer in your *Science Journal*.

2. INTERPRET DATA When is the average temperature highest for each city? Lowest?

3. INTERPRET DATA Describe the average weather pattern for each city. Be sure to include temperature and precipitation, and their relationship to the seasons.

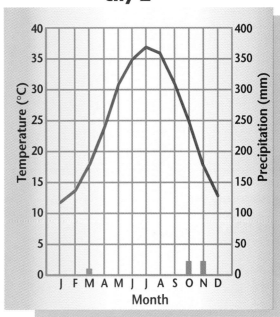

City 2

GOING FURTHER: Problem Solving

4. ANALYZE How would you go about making a graph of the weather patterns for your town?

―― Temperature (in Celsius)
■ Precipitation (in millimeters)

177

What Do Weather Patterns Tell You?

Weather changes from day to day. However, the weather in any area tends to follow a pattern throughout the year. For example, Fairbanks, Alaska, tends to have long, cold winters and short, cool summers. Miami, Florida, tends to have long, hot summers and short, cool winters.

When you make descriptions such as these, you are describing the **climate** (kli'mit) of a region. Climate is the average weather pattern of a region. One way to describe a region's climate is with a temperature-precipitation graph, as in the Explore Activity.

The climate of a region can also be described by some other factors, such as winds, distance from a coast, mountain ranges, and ocean currents. The *climatic zones* shown here take all these factors into account.

Another way to describe the climate of a region is by the plants that grow there, such as, grasslands or coniferous forests. Each kind of plant requires its own conditions for growth, such as amount of sunlight, precipitation and temperature.

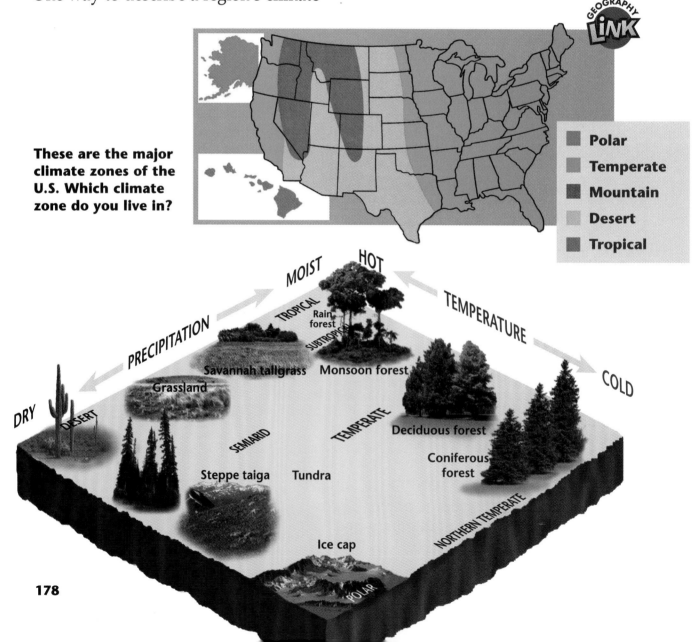

These are the major climate zones of the U.S. Which climate zone do you live in?

Polar
Temperate
Mountain
Desert
Tropical

DRY
PRECIPITATION
MOIST
HOT
TEMPERATURE
COLD

TROPICAL
Rain forest
SUBTROPICAL
Monsoon forest
Savannah tallgrass
Grassland
DESERT
SEMIARID
TEMPERATE
Deciduous forest
Coniferous forest
Steppe taiga
Tundra
Ice cap
NORTHERN TEMPERATE
POLAR

SKILL BUILDER

Skill: Making a Model

CLIMATES IN TWO AREAS

In this activity you will make a model of the soil conditions in the two cities on page 177. Use the information in the graph from the Explore Activity on page 177. The soil conditions you set up will model—or represent—the climates of the two cities.

page 177

MATERIALS

- stick-on notepaper
- marking pencil or pen
- 2 trays of dry soil
- spray bottle of water (like a plant mister)
- lamp
- thermometer
- *Science Journal*

PROCEDURES

1. MAKE A MODEL Put 3 cm of dry soil into each tray. Label one tray City 1 and the other tray City 2.

2. USE NUMBERS What do the bars on each graph in the Explore Activity represent? Make a list of the amounts given by the bars for each month for each city.

3. USE VARIABLES Model the yearly precipitation and temperature like this: Let 5 minutes equal 1 month. One squeeze of water sprayed on the tray equals 10 millimeters of precipitation. Every minute the lamp is on equals 20 degrees of temperature. That means that from 0 to 5 minutes is January. During January the City 2 tray gets no water and the lamp shines on it for $\frac{3}{4}$ minute. The City 1 tray gets 12 squeezes of water and the lamp shines on it for $2\frac{1}{4}$ minutes.

4. Model the two cities for all 12 months. Record your observations in your *Science Journal*.

CONCLUDE AND APPLY

1. COMPARE AND CONTRAST Examine the soil in the trays. Compare them at the same points in each year, for example, June and December. How do they differ?

2. EVALUATE How does your model show climates?

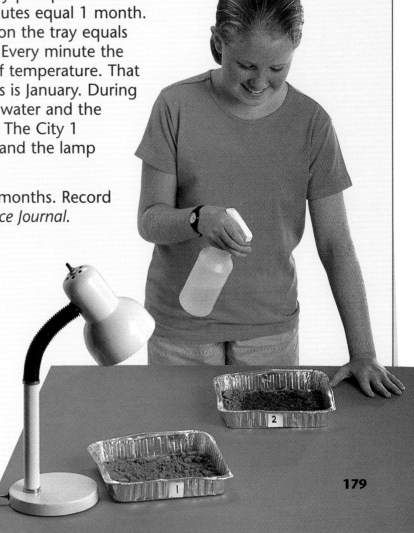

179

What Affects Climate?

Several things affect temperature and precipitation over a long period of time.

Latitude

One way to describe location is to tell the latitude of a place. Latitude is a measure of how far north or south a place is from the equator. The angle of insolation is different at different latitudes. As a result the temperatures are different at different latitudes.

- **Tropical Zone** Near the equator, temperatures are high all year. Rainfall is plentiful. At about 30° latitude in each hemisphere are deserts, areas of high temperatures and low precipitation.

- **Temperate Zones** In the middle latitudes, summers are warm and winters are cool or cold. Precipitation may be plentiful.

- **Polar Zones** At high latitudes, winters are long and cold. Summers are short and warm. Precipitation all year is low.

Bodies of Water

A glance at any globe shows that land and water are not evenly distributed. Most of the globe is covered with water. However, some places on a continent can be more than 1,000 miles from any large body of water.

Land and water heat and cool at different rates. Land heats up faster in the sunlight than water does. Land also cools off faster than water. As a result air temperatures over land are warmer in summer and cooler in winter than they are over oceans at the same latitude.

Winds and Ocean Currents

In Topic 4 you learned that wind patterns circle the globe. These patterns are not the day-to-day winds. Instead they are winds that blow continually above Earth's surface.

- **Wind Patterns** For example, just above and below the equator, the trade winds blow continually. In the middle latitudes are the westerlies. In the polar areas are the easterlies. Westerlies blow across the continental United States from west (the Pacific) to east. They bring warm, moist air to the west coast. They push air masses and fronts across the country.

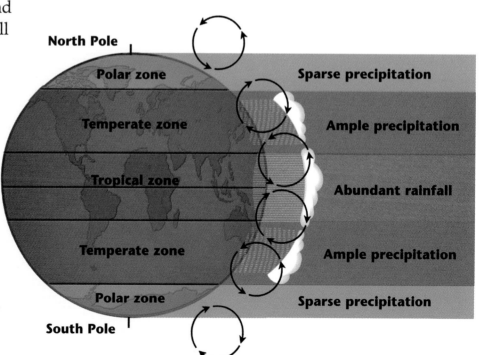

North Pole

Polar zone — Sparse precipitation

Temperate zone — Ample precipitation

Tropical zone — Abundant rainfall

Temperate zone — Ample precipitation

Polar zone — Sparse precipitation

South Pole

HOW ALTITUDE AFFECTS CLIMATE

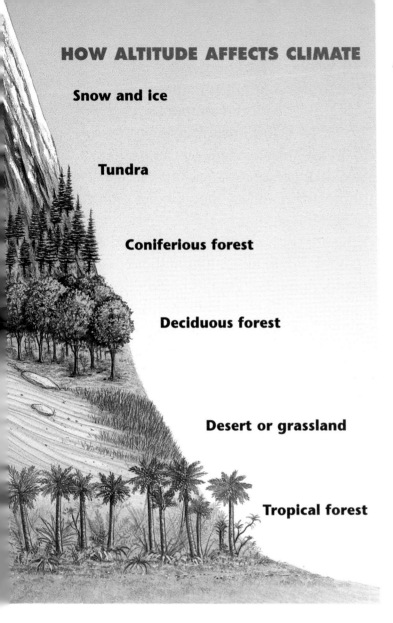

Snow and ice

Tundra

Coniferious forest

Deciduous forest

Desert or grassland

Tropical forest

- **Mountains** Along the base of a high mountain, you may find tropical plants growing. Halfway up you may find pine forests. At the mountain peaks, you will find permanent ice and snow. Mountain ranges affect climate, too. The Alps protect the Mediterranean coast from cold polar air. The Himalayas protect the lowlands of India from cold Siberian air. Mountain ranges also affect rain patterns. Often one side of the mountain gets lots of rain while the other side gets very little. Can you explain why?

- **Winds and Mountains** Global wind patterns can force air up along the side of a mountain. For example, warm moist air from the Pacific Ocean is blown up the side of the Sierra Nevada and the Cascades. As the air moves up, there is precipitation on the windward side. Having lost the moisture, dry air descends down the leeward side of the mountain.

- **Currents** These winds also move water across the surface of the ocean. As ocean water moves, it brings along warm or cool air from where it comes from to where it goes. A warm current, the Gulf Stream, flows up along the east coast. The California Current, a cool current, moves down along the west coast.

Altitude

Altitude is a measure of how high above sea level a place is. The higher a place is above sea level, the cooler its climate is.

Air passing over a mountain cools. Rain clouds may form and drop their moisture on that side of the mountain. Air reaching the other side is often dry.

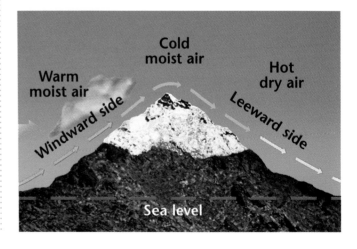

Cold moist air

Warm moist air

Hot dry air

Windward side

Leeward side

Sea level

How Does Earth Gain and Lose Energy?

Earth's climates depend a great deal on the Sun's energy. Earth absorbs heat from sunlight. It also gives out, or *radiates*, heat into space. Earth gains and loses.

If the amount of energy gained balances the energy lost, Earth is in **radiative** (rā′dē ā′tiv) **balance**. Then Earth's average temperature remains about the same. Earth's average temperature is about 14°C (59°F). A tip of the balance will cause Earth's average temperature to rise or fall.

The atmosphere plays an important role in Earth's radiative balance. If Earth had no atmosphere, it would be a lot like the Moon, which has no atmosphere. Daytime temperatures on the Moon soar to more than 100°C (212°F). Nighttime temperatures drop to 115°C (240°F) below zero.

Earth's atmosphere acts as a protective blanket. Clouds and dust in the atmosphere reflect about 30 percent of incoming sunlight back out into space. The atmosphere absorbs another 15–20 percent. Only about half of incoming sunlight reaches Earth's surface. This keeps surface temperatures from rising too high during the day.

At night Earth's surface and the atmosphere radiate heat. The atmosphere absorbs most of this heat. The atmosphere, in turn, radiates this heat, together with its own heat. Earth absorbs back almost half of what it lost. This keeps Earth from getting too cold at night.

EARTH'S ENERGY BUDGET

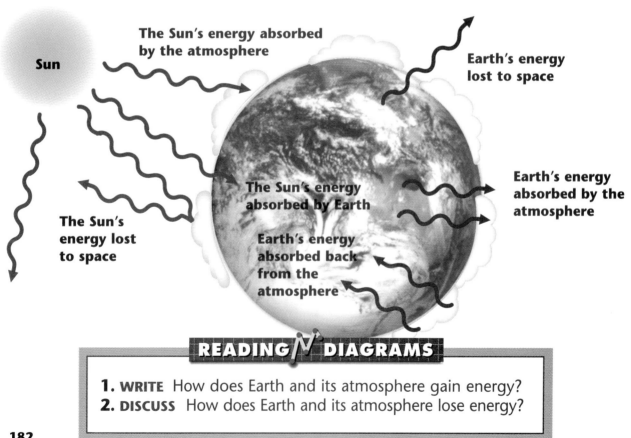

The Sun's energy absorbed by the atmosphere

Sun

Earth's energy lost to space

The Sun's energy lost to space

The Sun's energy absorbed by Earth

Earth's energy absorbed by the atmosphere

Earth's energy absorbed back from the atmosphere

READING N DIAGRAMS

1. WRITE How does Earth and its atmosphere gain energy?

2. DISCUSS How does Earth and its atmosphere lose energy?

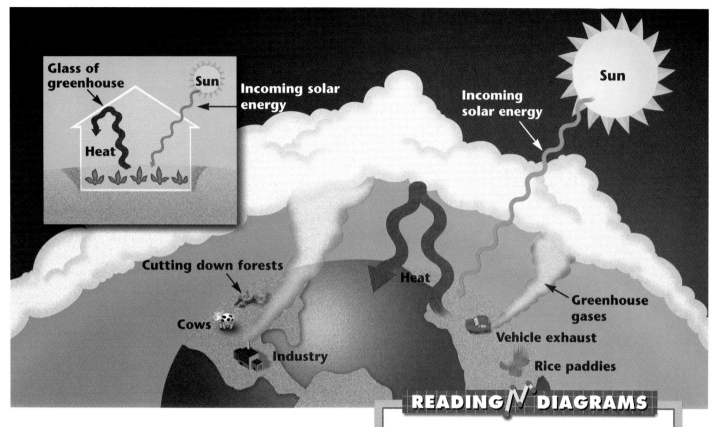

Glass of greenhouse

Sun

Incoming solar energy

Heat

Incoming solar energy

Sun

Cutting down forests

Heat

Cows

Industry

Greenhouse gases

Vehicle exhaust

Rice paddies

READING *N* **DIAGRAMS**

DISCUSS Write a description from this diagram of what causes the greenhouse effect.

How Is Earth Like a Greenhouse?

Why doesn't all of Earth's heat just go out into space? The atmosphere keeps Earth warmer than it would otherwise be. This is called the **greenhouse effect**. Earth's atmosphere acts somewhat like the glass in a greenhouse. In a greenhouse the glass lets sunlight in but does not let heat escape. This helps create a warm environment in which plants can flourish.

Earth's greenhouse effect is caused by just a few gases. These greenhouse gases make up only a tiny part of the air. The main greenhouse gases are *water vapor, carbon dioxide,* and *ozone.* Other gases also have an effect. These gases are *methane, nitrous oxide, chlorofluorocarbons (CFCs),* and *sulfur dioxide.*

Human activities are putting more and more greenhouse gases into the

atmosphere. Many scientists are worried that these gases may change Earth's climate. Even a small increase in these gases adds to the greenhouse effect, making our planet warmer.

Scientists are still examining and interpreting data in order to understand the greenhouse effect better.

Brain Power

Cans of items under pressure (hair sprays, paint sprays) indicate that they do not contain chlorofluoro-carbons. Why is this an important statement to list on a label?

Does Climate Change with Time?

There is much evidence that over long periods of time, Earth goes through warming and cooling trends. Warming and cooling are signs that Earth's radiative balance has shifted. What causes such shifts?

The shifts are caused by changes in sunlight. They are also caused by changes in the movements of air, water, landmasses, and Earth itself.

The Sun's Output

The amount of energy the Sun sends out changes. One clue to how the Sun's output may be changing comes from sunspots. Sunspots are dark areas that appear on the surface of the Sun. They appear dark because they are cooler than the surrounding regions. They appear to be "storms" on the Sun.

Sunspots have been observed for centuries. However, they are not permanent. They appear and disappear over several days time, or over several months.

Also there are times when there are many large sunspots. Such a high count is called a sunspot maximum. The last sunspot maximum was in 1989.

A sunspot maximum appears to happen about every 11 years. Scientists also date changes in Earth's temperatures about the same times. Around the time of a sunspot maximum, Earth's average temperatures have gone up. The pattern is not exact or complete. However, it has led some scientists to suggest droughts, rainfalls, and very cold winters might be related to times when sunspots are very numerous or very few.

Brain Power

When might the next sunspot maximum occur?

The Sun's surface

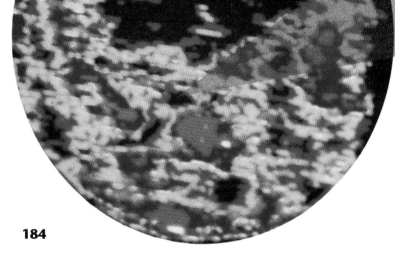

Sunspot

When they appear sunspots can affect radio and TV broadcasts on Earth. Can they also affect temperatures?

Ocean Currents

How do the oceans help move Earth's heat around? Ocean currents act like huge conveyor belts, carrying heat from the equator to the poles. Changes in the speed and direction of these currents could explain sudden and long-term climate changes.

The continents have changed their positions over time. In fact the continents and ocean bottoms are still moving very gradually. Their climates are likely to change with their locations.

Volcanoes

When volcanoes erupt they send dust and gases into the atmosphere. Atmospheric dust can block sunlight, causing cooling. In the past, eruptions were more frequent. The dust from all of those eruptions may have caused enough cooling to trigger ice ages. Volcanic eruptions are not as common today as they were in the past. While eruptions still cause cooling, they probably don't affect long-term climate as much as in the past.

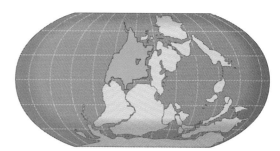

300 Million Years Ago

Present

Do you think the ocean currents were the same 300 million years ago as they are today? Changes in ocean currents would profoundly affect climates.

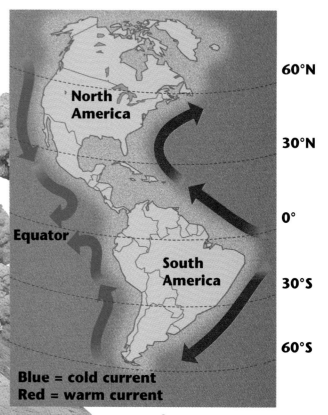

Blue = cold current
Red = warm current

Some currents affecting the Western Hemisphere today

Brain Power

What difference does it make if Earth's climate gets just a couple of degrees warmer or cooler than it is today?

How Can Climate Affect You?

How do you deal with cold weather? Cold weather cools the surface of the body. The body responds by circulating warm blood faster to counteract the cooling. The heart pumps faster. Blood pressure increases and puts a strain on the heart.

Cold Climates

How can you stay warm in cold weather? Use proper clothing and shelter. Clothing traps body heat to warm the air close to your body. Cold-weather clothes are often made with materials that trap air between loose fibers. Your body heats the trapped air, and soon a thin, warm layer of air surrounds you.

Hot Climates

In hot, dry climates, the main health problem is water loss. Heating the body triggers sweating. When sweat evaporates it cools the skin. However, if you don't drink enough water, your body eventually stops sweating. No sweat, no cooling. Body temperature rises. This can cause *hyperthermia* (overheating), which can be fatal.

Clothing can help you deal with the heat. Leaving your skin bare can make you feel hotter. That's because your skin absorbs the full energy of sunlight. It also increases your risk of getting skin cancer. Light-colored fabric protects the skin and reflects a lot of the sunlight. Loose clothing lets air circulate so sweat can evapo-rate and cool the body.

How to Dress in Hot Weather

Light-colored, loose clothing that protects you from the Sun and lets your skin breathe

•

Sun hat

•

Sunscreen

How to Dress in Cold Weather

Protect nose and ears on blustery, cold days

•

Keep hands, head, and feet warm

•

Dress in layers to trap body heat

Crops in the Past

Climate has been affecting how food is produced, since farming began, about 6,000 years ago. At that time average temperatures were about 2°C (4°F) warmer than today. There was also more rainfall. Crops thrived in the warm, moist climate. About A.D. 200 the climate started to cool. Crops failed.

By A.D. 900–1100, temperatures had warmed up again. However, by 1300 the climate had started to cool again. Between 1450 and 1850, there was a cold period called the Little Ice Age. There were many harsh winters. Stretches of cold, wet summers in the 1590s, the 1690s, and the 1810s caused crops to fail and led to famines.

Crops Since 1900

Since 1900 the average temperature has increased by about 0.5°C (1°F). A drought during the 1920s–1940s led to the Dust Bowl days. Millions of acres of United States farmland dried out. Crops failed. Farmers went broke trying to pay their bills.

You may experience several climates in your lifetime. You may travel to faraway places with climates different from your own. In large states like Texas or California, you can experience many climates in different parts of the state.

When you become an adult, your job may bring you to climates different from your present climate. You may enjoy one climate more than another. You may choose to live in a climate different from the one you are used to.

Winter fairs were held on the Thames River in London during the Little Ice Age.

REVIEW

1. What is climate? What are the main factors that are used to describe the climate of an area?

2. **MAKE A MODEL** How can you make models to show a dry climate and a moist climate?

3. Why are climates different at different places on Earth?

4. What is the greenhouse effect?

5. **CRITICAL THINKING** *Analyze* Do you think people can live in all climates? Explain your answer.

WHY IT MATTERS THINK ABOUT IT
What is the climate like in your area?

WHY IT MATTERS WRITE ABOUT IT
Choose a climate that is different from your own. How do people in that climate live differently from you?

A WARMER WORLD?

"Our climate is definitely warming up," says Tom Karl, Senior Scientist at the National Climatic Data Center in North Carolina. It's the world's largest collector of weather data—its computers have more than 150 years of information. Every day 18 million more pages of weather data come in!

Karl and his team studied worldwide temperatures between 1900 and 1997. They discovered that 1997 was the warmest year since 1900 and that 9 of the past 11 years have been warmer than average!

Karl believes the cause is probably an increase in greenhouse gases. Not everyone agrees. In 1997 most state climate experts said global warming is natural, caused by changes in the Sun and in Earth's orbit. They added that Earth's climate would change even if no one lived on the planet!

DISCUSSION STARTER

How do you think we can identify the cause of global warming?

To learn more about global warming, visit *www.mhschool.com/science* and enter the keyword WARM.

inter**NET** CONNECTION

SCIENCE WORDS

air mass p.150

climate p.178

cold front p.152

front p.151

greenhouse
effect p.183

hurricane p.166

radiative
balance p.182

storm surge p.168

tornado p.164

warm front p.152

USING SCIENCE WORDS
Number a paper from 1 to 10. Fill in 1 to 5 with words from the list above.

1. The ___?___ may be making Earth warmer.

2. A great rise of sea level at a shore due to a hurricane is a(n)___?___.

3. A dangerous storm that forms over warm ocean waters is a(n) ___?___.

4. A(n) ___?___ forms when cold air moves in under a warm air mass.

5. The average weather pattern of a region is its ___?___.

6–10. Pick five words from the list above that were not used in 1 to 5, and use each in a sentence.

UNDERSTANDING SCIENCE IDEAS

11. What is the difference between a cold front and a warm front?

12. How is the weather a warm front brings different from the weather a cold front brings?

13. What are two things that can affect climate?

14. What happens when a front stays over a region for a long time?

15. How are tornadoes and hurricanes different?

USING IDEAS AND SKILLS

16. **READING SKILL: SEQUENCE OF EVENTS** Pick a severe storm. Describe how it forms.

17. Why is the severe storm you described in number 16 dangerous?

18. How are tornadoes often related to thunderstorms?

19. **MAKE A MODEL** What if your area was to get twice as much rain as usual for the next ten years? How would you make a model of your climate as it is now? How would you adjust it to study the effect of the extra rainfall?

20. **THINKING LIKE A SCIENTIST** Do you think that Earth is getting warmer? State and explain your hypothesis. Describe what you might do to test your ideas.

PROBLEMS and PUZZLES

Forecast Accuracy Write down a weather forecaster's five-day forecast. Check the weather each day over the five days. Determine a way to rate how accurate the forecast turned out to be. Repeat several times. Why isn't it ever competely accurate?

SCIENCE WORDS

air pressure p.105

atmosphere p.104

climate p.178

condensation p.115

convection

  cell p.136

Coriolis effect p.138

evaporation p.112

front p.151

greenhouse

  effect p.183

humidity p.112

hurricane p.166

precipitation p.124

thunderstorm

  p.162

tornado p.164

troposphere p.104

USING SCIENCE WORDS

Number a paper from 1 to 10. Beside each number write the word or words that best complete the sentence.

1. The blanket of gases that surrounds Earth is the __?__.

2. Evaporation increases the __?__ in the air.

3. Evaporation is the opposite of __?__.

4. Rain, sleet, and snow are all forms of __?__.

5. Air rises and sinks in a(n) __?__.

6. The curved paths of winds are caused by __?__.

7. The boundary between two masses of air with different temperatures is called a(n) __?__.

8. A violent spinning wind that moves in a narrow path is a __?__.

9. The normal weather pattern of a place is called its __?__.

10. Earth's atmosphere tends to trap heat because of the __?__.

UNDERSTANDING SCIENCE IDEAS

Write 11 to 15. For each number write the letter for the best answer. You may wish to use the hints provided.

11. On a hot day, a lake is likely to be
    a. cooler than nearby land
    b. hotter than nearby land
    c. the same temperature as the land
    d. the cause of the heat
    (Hint: Read page 103.)

12. Water drops that collect on a cold glass of lemonade come from
    a. the lemonade
    b. the air
    c. a puddle
    d. the glass itself
    (Hint: Read page 112.)

13. The water cycle describes how water
    a. flows upstream
    b. spins in a tornado
    c. changes form
    d. heats up the atmosphere
    (Hint: Read pages 126–127.)

14. Statistical weather forecasts are based on
    a. the kinds of fronts moving out of an area
    b. severe storms
    c. the chance of a weather pattern repeating itself
    d. weather station symbols
    (Hint: Read pages 148–149.)

15. Earth gets its heat from
    a. trees
    b. convection
    c. greenhouses
    d. the Sun
    (Hint: Read page 182.)

USING IDEAS AND SKILLS

16. The troposphere is different from other layers of the atmosphere. What takes place there as a result of this difference?

17. Why does the air temperature usually increase between sunrise and noon?

18. How does water vapor get into the air?

19. What is fog, and how does it form?

20. How is air pressure related to air temperature?

21. USE NUMBERS What does a weather station model tell you?

22. What is the purpose of a weather station?

23. What causes thunderstorms?

THINKING LIKE A SCIENTIST

24. MAKE A MODEL You use sand in a tray to model climates. Why would you build a model using simple things that do not seem to have anything to do with a topic?

25. What is the climate like where you live?

WRITING IN YOUR JOURNAL

SCIENCE IN YOUR LIFE
How does the weather affect your daily activities? Is there a difference between what you do on rainy days and what you do on clear, sunny days?

PRODUCT ADS
What products are advertised to protect you from the weather in the winter? In the summer? What is each product supposed to do? Are the products as good as the ads say? Explain.

HOW SCIENTISTS WORK
In this unit you learned about how weather data is collected. How do you think scientists decide what is the best kind of data to collect?

Design your own Experiment

How much does humidity change over the course of a day? To find out, design an experiment using a glass of cold water, a thermometer, and a timer. Check your experiment with your teacher before you perform it.

*inter*NET CONNECTION

For more help in reviewing this unit, visit *www.mhschool.com/science*

PROBLEMS and PUZZLES

Heat Index

When the temperature and the relative humidity are both high, the air temperature may "feel" greater than what the thermometer reads. The temperature that you feel is called the *heat index*.

Find 90°F on the graph. Move your finger across the 90°F line to where it meets the 70% relative humidity line. At the point where the two lines meet, the heat index is 105°F. As you move your finger right to higher relative humidities, the heat index gets higher.

Find the heat index for any temperatures 80°F and over at relative humidities over 40% on the graph. The greater the heat index, the darker the shaded portions of the graph, the greater the chance of the heat affecting your health. How can knowing the heat index help you?

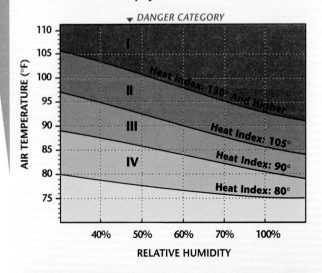

Wind and Clouds

Is there a relationship between how cloudy it is and the wind (such as wind direction or speed)? Design a way to tell the wind direction each day. Keep a daily record of

• cloud cover
• wind direction
• wind speed (using the Beauford scale)
• fronts moving through your area (by listening to local weather reports)

Put this information together over a period of several weeks to try to find a relationship.

Soggy Cereal Caper

Tanya left a box of Corn Roasties cereal open on an 80°F July day when the relative humidity was 80%. The cereal got soggy overnight. In December Tanya did the same thing when the temperature was 20°F and the relative humidity was also 80%. This time the cereal did not get soggy. Can you explain what made the cereal soggy in July but not in December? How could you test your answer?

REFERENCE SECTION

DIAGRAM BUILDERS

Building the Water Cycle

A cycle is a number of events or processes that happen in a given order over and over again. For example, Monday follows Sunday, Tuesday follows Monday, and so on, over and over again. Every drop of water is part of the water cycle. The water cycle is the continuous movement of water between Earth's surface and the air. **What happens to water in this cycle?**

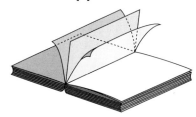

BASE

To find out, look at the diagram on the facing page. You can see many processes all happening at the same time. You can study this cycle one process at a time by lifting up all the plastic overlays (1, 2, 3). Look at the page beneath, the base. **What sources of water do you see? What source of energy do you see?**

OVERLAY 1

1 Now drop overlay 1 onto the base.
What happens to liquid water? Why?

OVERLAY 2

2 Now drop overlay 2 onto overlay 1.
What process follows those shown on the first overlay? What happens to the water?

OVERLAY 3

3 Now drop overlay 3 onto overlay 2.
What processes complete the cycle?

SUMMARIZE

What can happen to a drop of water that is in the ground, in the leaf of a plant, or at the surface of a body of water?

BASE: Start with water on and in the ground.

DIAGRAM BUILDERS
Activities

1 Make a Diagram

What cycles can you describe that take place over a week, a month, or a year? Make a diagram to show how the parts of the cycles are arranged.

2 Write About a Main Idea

Does a cycle have a beginning? An end? Write out your idea. Use the Water Cycle diagram to support your idea.

3 Make a Model

Use art materials, natural materials, and any other supplies to make a model of the water cycle. How might you make a working model that shows at least some of the processes of the cycle?

REFERENCE SECTION

HANDBOOK

This bottle of juice has a volume of 1 liter.

That is a little more than 1 quart.

She can walk 20 meters in 5 seconds.

That means her speed is 4 meters per second.

Table of Measurements

SI (INTERNATIONAL SYSTEM) OF UNITS

Temperature

Water freezes at 0°C and boils at 100°C.

Length and Distance

1,000 meters = 1 kilometer
100 centimeters = 1 meter
10 millimeters = 1 centimeter

Volume

1,000 milliliters = 1 liter
1 cubic centimeter = 1 milliliter

Mass

1,000 grams = 1 kilogram

ENGLISH SYSTEM OF UNITS

Temperature

Water freezes at 32°F and boils at 212°F.

Length and Distance

5,280 feet = 1 mile
3 feet = 1 yard
12 inches = 1 foot

Volume of Fluids [C head]

4 quarts = 1 gallon
2 pints = 1 quart
2 cups = 1 pint
8 fluid ounces = 1 cup

Weight

2,000 pounds = 1 ton
16 ounces = 1 pound

In the Classroom

The most important part of doing any experiment is doing it safely. You can be safe by paying attention to your teacher and doing your work carefully. Here are some other ways to stay safe while you do experiments.

Before the Experiment

- Read all of the directions. Make sure you understand them. When you see be sure to follow the safety rule.

- Listen to your teacher for special safety directions. If you don't understand something, ask for help.

During the Experiment

- Wear safety goggles when your teacher tells you to wear them and whenever you see .
- Wear a safety apron if you work with anything messy or anything that might spill.
- If you spill something, wipe it up right away or ask your teacher for help.
- Tell your teacher if something breaks. If glass breaks do not clean it up yourself.

- Keep your hair and clothes away from open flames. Tie back long hair and roll up long sleeves.
- Be careful around a hot plate. Know when it is on and when it is off. Remember that the plate stays hot for a few minutes after you turn it off.
- Keep your hands dry around electrical equipment.
- Don't eat or drink anything during the experiment.

After the Experiment

- Put equipment back the way your teacher tells you.
- Dispose of things the way your teacher tells you.
- Clean up your work area and wash your hands.

In the Field

- Always be accompanied by a trusted adult—like your teacher or a parent or guardian.
- Never touch animals or plants without the adult's approval. The animal might bite. The plant might be poison ivy or another dangerous plant.

Responsibility

Acting safely is one way to be responsible. You can also be responsible by treating animals, the environment, and each other with respect in the class and in the field.

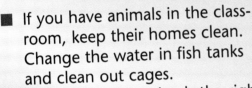

Treat Living Things with Respect

- If you have animals in the classroom, keep their homes clean. Change the water in fish tanks and clean out cages.
- Feed classroom animals the right amount of food.
- Give your classroom animals enough space.
- When you observe animals, don't hurt them or disturb their homes.
- Find a way to care for animals while school is on vacation.

Treat the Environment with Respect

- Do not pick flowers.
- Do not litter, including gum and food.
- If you see litter, ask your teacher if you can pick it up.
- Recycle materials used in experiments. Ask your teacher what materials can be recycled instead of thrown away. These might include plastics, aluminum, and newspapers.

Treat Each Other with Respect

- Use materials carefully around others so that people don't get hurt or get stains on their clothes.
- Be careful not to bump people when they are doing experiments. Do not disturb or damage their experiments.
- If you see that people are having trouble with an experiment, help them.

Use a Hand Lens

You use a hand lens to magnify an object, or make the object look larger. With a hand lens, you can see details that would be hard to see without the hand lens.

Magnify a Piece of Cereal

1. Place a piece of your favorite cereal on a flat surface. Look at the cereal carefully. Draw a picture of it.
2. Look at the cereal through the large lens of a hand lens. Move the lens toward or away from the cereal until it looks larger and in focus. Draw a picture of the cereal as you see it through the hand lens. Fill in details that you did not see before.
3. Look at the cereal through the smaller lens, which will magnify the cereal even more. If you notice more details, add them to your drawing.
4. Repeat this activity using objects you are studying in science. It might be a rock, some soil, or a seed.

Observe Seeds in a Petri Dish

Can you observe a seed as it sprouts? You can if it's in a petri dish. A petri dish is a shallow, clear, round dish with a cover.

1. Line the sides and bottom of a petri dish with a double layer of filter paper or paper towel. You may have to cut the paper to make it fit.
2. Sprinkle water on the paper to wet it.
3. Place three or four radish seeds on the wet paper in different areas of the dish. Put the lid on the dish, and keep it in a warm place.
4. Observe the seeds every day for a week. Use a hand lens to look for a tiny root pushing through the seed. Record how long it takes each seed to sprout.

Use a Microscope

Hand lenses make objects look several times larger. A microscope, however, can magnify an object to look hundreds of times larger.

Examine Salt Grains

1. Look at the photograph to learn the different parts of your microscope.
2. Place the microscope on a flat surface. Always carry a microscope with both hands. Hold the arm with one hand, and put your other hand beneath the base.
3. Move the mirror so that it reflects light up toward the stage. Never point the mirror directly at the Sun or a bright light.
4. Place a few grains of salt on the slide. Put the slide under the stage clips. Be sure that the salt grains you are going to examine are over the hole in the stage.
5. Look through the eyepiece. Turn the focusing knob slowly until the salt grains come into focus.
6. Draw what the grains look like through the microscope.
7. Look at other objects through the microscope. Try a piece of leaf, a human hair, or a pencil mark.

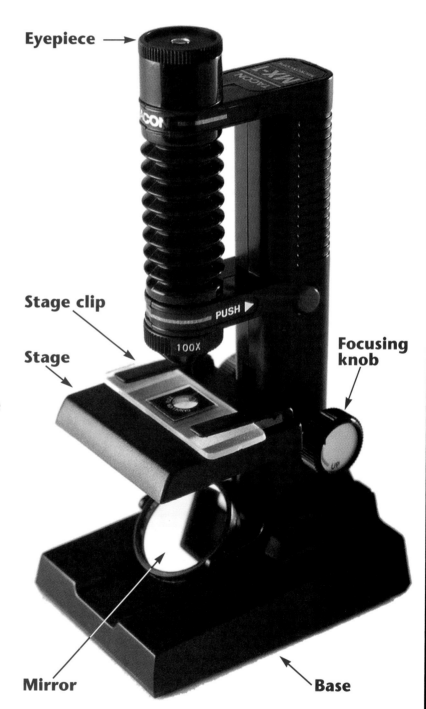

Eyepiece

Stage clip

Stage

Focusing knob

Mirror

Base

Use a Collecting Net

You can use a collecting net to catch insects and observe them. You can try catching an insect in midair, but you might have better luck waiting for it to land on a plant. Put the net over the whole plant. Then you can place the insect in a jar with holes in the lid.

Use a Compass

You use a compass to find directions. A compass is a small, thin magnet that swings freely, like a spinner in a board game. One end of the magnet always points north. This end is the magnet's north pole. How does a compass work?

1. Place the compass on a surface that is not made of magnetic material, such as a wooden table or a sidewalk.

2. Find the magnet's north pole. The north pole is marked in some way, usually with a color or an arrowhead.
3. Notice the letters *N*, *E*, *S*, and *W* on the compass. These letters stand for the directions north, east, south, and west. When the magnet stops swinging, turn the compass so that the *N* lines up with the north pole of the magnet.
4. Face to the north. Then face to the east, to the south, and to the west.
5. Repeat this activity by holding the compass in your hand and then at different places indoors and outdoors.

Use a Telescope

You make most observations for science class during the day. Some things are observed best at night—like the Moon and the stars.

You can observe the Moon and the stars simply by looking up into a clear night sky. However, it's hard to see much detail on the Moon, such as craters and mountains. Also you can see only a tiny fraction of the stars and other objects that are actually in the sky. A telescope improves those observations.

A telescope uses lenses or mirrors to gather light and magnify objects. You can see much greater detail of the Moon's surface with a telescope than with just your eyes. A telescope gathers light better than your eyes can. With a telescope you can see stars that are too faint to see with just your eyes. See for yourself how a telescope can improve your observations.

1. Look at the Moon in the night sky, and draw a picture of what you see. Draw as many details as you can.
2. Point a telescope toward the Moon. Look through the eyepiece of the telescope. Move the telescope until you see the Moon. Turn the knob until the Moon comes into focus.

3. Draw a picture of what you see, including as many details as you can. Compare your two pictures.
4. Find the brightest star in the sky. Notice if there are any other stars near it.
5. Point a telescope toward the bright star. Look through the eyepiece and turn the knob until the stars come into focus. Move the telescope until you find the bright star.
6. Can you see stars through the telescope that you cannot see with just your eyes?

Objective lens

Eyepiece lens
Focusing knob

HANDBOOK

Use a Camera, Tape Recorder, Map, and Compass

Camera

You can use a camera to record what you observe in nature. When taking photographs keep these tips in mind.

1. Hold the camera steady. Gently press the shutter button so that you do not jerk the camera.
2. Try to take pictures with the Sun at your back. Then your pictures will be bright and clear.
3. Don't get too close to the subject. Without a special lens, the picture could turn out blurry.
4. Be patient. If you are taking a picture of an animal, you may have to wait for the animal to appear.

Tape Recorder

You can record observations on a tape recorder. This is sometimes better than writing notes because, with a tape recorder, you can record your observations at the exact time you are making them. Later you can listen to the tape and write down your observations.

Use a Map and a Compass

When you are busy observing nature, it might be easy to get lost. You can use a map of the area and a compass to find your way. Here are some tips.

1. Lightly mark on the map your starting place. It might be the place where the bus parked.
2. Always know where you are on the map compared to your starting place. Watch for landmarks on the map, such as a river, a pond, trails, or buildings.
3. Use the map and compass to find special places to observe, such as a pond. Look at the map to see what direction the place is from you. Hold the compass to see where that direction is.
4. Use your map and compass with a friend.

HANDBOOK

Length

Find Length with a Ruler

1. Look at this section of a ruler. Each centimeter is divided into 10 millimeters. How long is the paper clip?
2. The length of the paper clip is 3 centimeters plus 2 millimeters. You can write this length as 3.2 centimeters.
3. Place the ruler on your desk. Lay a pencil against the ruler so that one end of the pencil lines up with the left edge of the ruler. Record the length of the pencil.
4. Trade your pencil with a classmate. Measure and record the length of each other's pencil. Compare your answers.

1 centimeter = 10 millimeters

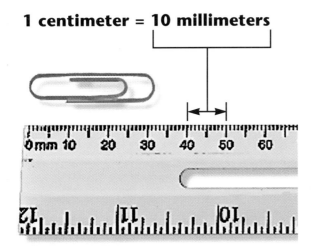

Find Length with a Meterstick

1. Line up the meterstick with the left edge of the chalkboard. Make a chalk mark on the board at the right end of the meterstick.
2. Move the meterstick so that the left edge lines up with the chalk mark. Keep the stick level. Make another mark on the board at the right end of the meterstick.
3. Continue to move the meterstick and make chalk marks until the meterstick meets or overlaps the right edge of the board.
4. Record the length of the chalkboard in centimeters by adding all the measurements you've made. Remember, a meterstick has 100 centimeters.

Measuring Area

Area is the amount of surface something covers. To find the area of a rectangle, multiply the rectangle's length by its width. For example, the rectangle here is 3 centimeters long and 2 centimeters wide. Its area is 3 cm x 2 cm = 6 square centimeters. You write the area as 6 cm².

1. Find the area of your science book. Measure the book's length to the nearest centimeter. Measure its width.
2. Multiply the book's length by its width. Remember to put the answer in cm².

3 cm

◄2 cm►

R11

Time

You use timing devices to measure how long something takes to happen. Some timing devices you use in science are a clock with a second hand and a stopwatch. Which one is more accurate?

Comparing a Clock and Stopwatch

1. Look at a clock with a second hand. The second hand is the hand that you can see moving. It measures seconds.

2. Get an egg timer with falling sand or some device like a wind-up toy that runs down after a certain length of time. When the second hand of the clock points to 12, tell your partner to start the egg timer. Watch the clock while the sand in the egg timer is falling.

3. When the sand stops falling, count how many seconds it took. Record this measurement. Repeat the activity, and compare the two measurements.

4. Switch roles with your partner.

5. Look at a stopwatch. Click the button on the top right. This starts the time. Click the button again. This stops the time. Click the button on the top left. This sets the stopwatch back to zero. Notice that the stopwatch tells time in minutes, seconds, and hundredths of a second.

6. Repeat the activity in steps 1–3, using the stopwatch instead of a clock. Make sure the stopwatch is set to zero. Click the top right button to start timing the reading. Click it again when the sand stops falling. Make sure you and your partner time each other twice.

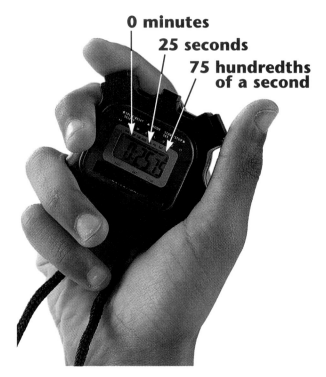

0 minutes
25 seconds
75 hundredths of a second

More About Time

1. Use the stopwatch to time how long it takes an ice cube to melt under cold running water. How long does an ice cube take to melt under warm running water?

2. Match each of these times with the action you think took that amount of time.

a. 0:00:14:55
b. 0:24:39:45
c. 2:10:23:00

1. A Little League baseball game
2. Saying the Pledge of Allegiance
3. Recess

Volume

Volume is the amount of space something takes up. If you've ever helped bake a cake or do other cooking, you might have measured the volume of water, vegetable oil, or melted butter. In science you usually measure the volume of liquids by using beakers and graduated cylinders. These containers are marked in milliliters (mL).

Measure the Volume of a Liquid

1. Look at the beaker and at the graduated cylinder. The beaker has marks for each 25 mL up to 200 mL. The graduated cylinder has marks for each 1 mL up to 100 mL.
2. The surface of the water in the graduated cylinder curves up at the sides. You measure the volume by reading the height of the water at the flat part. What is the volume of water in the graduated cylinder? How much water is in the beaker? They both contain 75 mL of water.

3. Pour 50 mL of water from a pitcher into a graduated cylinder. The water should be at the 50-mL mark on the graduated cylinder. If you go over the mark, pour a little water back into the pitcher.
4. Pour the 50 mL of water into a beaker.
5. Repeat steps 3 and 4 using 30 mL, 45 mL, and 25 mL of water.
6. Measure the volume of water you have in the beaker. Do you have about the same amount of water as your classmates?

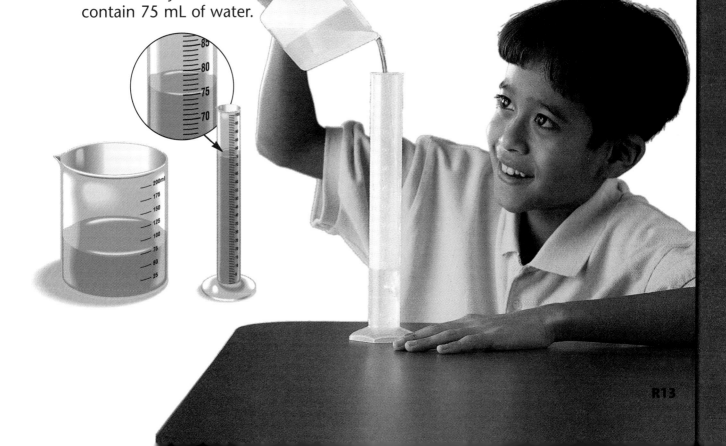

Mass

Mass is the amount of matter an object has. You use a balance to measure mass. To find the mass of an object, you balance it with objects whose masses you know. Let's find the mass of a box of crayons.

Measure the Mass of a Box of Crayons

1. Place the balance on a flat, level surface. Check that the two pans are empty and clean.
2. Make sure the empty pans are balanced with each other. The pointer should point to the middle mark. If it does not, move the slider a little to the right or left to balance the pans.
3. Gently place a box of crayons on the left pan. This pan will drop lower.
4. Add masses to the right pan until the pans are balanced.
5. Add the numbers on the masses that are in the right pan. The total is the mass of the box of crayons, in grams. Record this number. After the number write a *g* for "grams."

Predict the Mass of More Crayons

1. Leave the box of crayons and the masses on the balance.
2. Get two more crayons. If you put them in the pan with the box of crayons, what do you think the mass of all the crayons will be? Record what you predict the total mass will be.
3. Check your prediction. Gently place the two crayons in the left pan. Add masses to the right pan until the pans are balanced.
4. Add the numbers on the masses as you did before. Record this number. How close is it to your prediction?

More About Mass

What was the mass of all your crayons? It was probably less than 100 grams. What would happen if you replaced the crayons with a pineapple? You may not have enough masses to balance the pineapple. It has a mass of about 1,000 grams. That's the same as 1 kilogram because *kilo* means "1,000."

1. How many kilograms do all these masses add up to?
2. Which of these objects have a mass greater than 1 kilogram?
   a. large dog
   b. robin
   c. desktop computer
   d. calculator
   e. whole watermelon

MAKE MEASUREMENTS

Weight/Force

You use a spring scale to measure weight. An object has weight because the force of gravity pulls down on the object. Therefore, weight is a force. Weight is measured in newtons (N) like all forces.

Measure the Weight of an Object

1. Look at your spring scale to see how many newtons it measures. See how the measurements are divided. The spring scale shown here measures up to 5 N. It has a mark for every 0.1 N.
2. Hold the spring scale by the top loop. Put the object to be measured on the bottom hook. If the object will not stay on the hook, place it in a net bag. Then hang the bag from the hook.
3. Let go of the object slowly. It will pull down on a spring inside the scale. The spring is connected to a pointer. The pointer on the spring scale shown here is a small bar.
4. Wait for the pointer to stop moving. Read the number of newtons next to the pointer. This is the object's weight. The mug in the picture weighs 4 N.

More About Spring Scales

You probably weigh yourself by standing on a bathroom scale. This is a spring scale. The force of your body stretches a spring inside the scale. The dial on the scale is probably marked in pounds—the English unit of weight. One pound is equal to about 4.5 newtons.

Here are some other spring scales you may have seen.

Temperature

You use a thermometer to measure temperature—how hot or cold something is. A thermometer is made of a thin tube with colored liquid inside. When the liquid gets warmer, it expands and moves up the tube. When the liquid gets cooler, it contracts and moves down the tube. You may have seen most temperatures measured in degrees Fahrenheit (°F). Scientists measure temperature in degrees Celsius (°C).

°F   °C

Water boils

Room temperature

Water freezes

Read a Thermometer

1. Look at the thermometer shown here. It has two scales—a Fahrenheit scale and a Celsius scale. Every 20 degrees on the Fahrenheit scale has a number. Every 10 degrees on the Celsius scale has a number.

2. What is the temperature shown on the thermometer? At what temperature does water freeze? Give your answers in °F and in °C.

What Is Convection?

1. Fill a large beaker about two-thirds full of cool water. Find the temperature of the water by holding a thermometer in the water. Do not let the bulb at the bottom of the thermometer touch the sides or bottom of the beaker.

2. Keep the thermometer in the water until the liquid in the tube stops moving—about a minute. Read and record the temperature in °C.

3. Sprinkle a little fish food on the surface of the water in the beaker. Do not knock the beaker, and most of the food will stay on top.

4. Carefully place the beaker on a hot plate. A hot plate is a small electric stove. Plug in the hot plate, and turn the control knob to a middle setting.

5. After a minute measure the temperature of water near the bottom of the beaker. At the same time, a classmate should measure the temperature of water near the top of the beaker. Record these temperatures. Is water near the bottom of the beaker heating up faster than near the top?

6. As the water heats up, notice what happens to the fish food. How do you know that warmer water at the bottom of the beaker rises and cooler water at the top sinks?

Weather

What information is included in a weather report? You might think of temperature, cloud cover, wind speed, amount of rainfall, and so on. Various instruments are used to measure these parts of the weather. Some of them are shown here.

Barometer

A barometer measures air pressure. Most barometers are like the one shown here. It contains a flat metal can with most of the air removed. When air pressure increases (rises), the air pushes more on the can. A pointer that is attached to the can moves toward a higher number on the scale. When air pressure decreases (falls), the air pushes less on the can. The pointer moves toward a lower number on the scale.

29.73 inches ⟶

Notice that the barometer above measures air pressure in inches and in centimeters. The long arrow points to the current air pressure, which is 29.73 inches of mercury. That means the air pushing down on liquid mercury in a dish would force the mercury 29.73 inches up a tube, as the drawing shows. What is the air pressure in centimeters?

Follow these steps when you use a barometer.

1. Look at the current air pressure reading marked by the long arrow.
2. Turn the knob on the front of the barometer so the short arrow points to the current pressure reading.
3. Check the barometer several times a day to see if the pressure is rising, falling, or staying the same.

Rain Gauge

A rain gauge measures how much rain falls. This instrument is simply a container that collects water. It has one or more scales for measuring the amount of rain.

The rain gauge shown here has been collecting rain throughout the day. How much rain fell in inches? In centimeters?

Weather Vane

A weather vane indicates wind direction. A weather vane is basically an arrow that is free to spin on a pole. Wind pushes on the widest part of the arrow—the tail—so that the arrow points to the direction that the wind is coming from. Letters on the weather vane show directions. If the vane doesn't have letters, you can tell direction with a compass. What direction is the wind coming from in the picture?

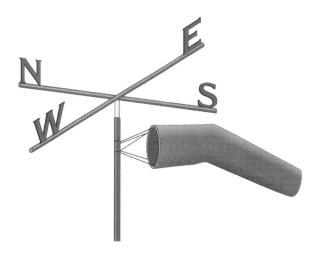

Windsock

A windsock also indicates wind direction. You may have seen windsocks at airports. Windsocks are usually large and bright orange so that pilots can easily see which way the wind is blowing. The large opening of the windsock faces the wind. The narrow part of the windsock points in the direction that the wind is blowing. Which way is the wind blowing in the picture?

Anemometer

An anemometer measures wind speed. It is usually made of three shallow cones, or cups, that spin on an axle. The wind makes the cups and axle spin. The axle is attached to a dial that indicates wind speed. The faster the wind blows, the faster the cups turn.

Cycles

Much of what happens in nature happens in cycles. A cycle is a process that keeps repeating itself. For example, the movement of water through the environment is a cycle. Water evaporates from the ground, rises into the air, condenses into clouds, and falls back to Earth as rain or snow. Once on the ground, it might evaporate again, and the cycle continues.

The drawings below illustrate other natural cycles. See if you can describe each cycle shown.

Think about some cycles in your own life—things that you do over and over again on a regular basis. Describe a daily cycle from your experience. Describe a weekly cycle from your experience.

Make Graphs to Organize Data

When you do an experiment in science, you collect information. To find out what your information means, you can organize it into graphs. There are many kinds of graphs.

Circle Graphs

A circle graph is helpful to show how a complete set of data is divided into parts. The circle graph here shows how water is used in the United States. What is the single largest use of water?

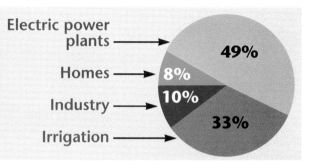

Electric power plants —→ 49%
Homes —→ 8%
Industry —→ 10%
Irrigation —→ 33%

Bar Graphs

A bar graph uses bars to show information. For example, what if you do an experiment by wrapping wire around a nail and connecting the ends of the wire to a battery? The nail then becomes a magnet that can pick up paper clips. The graph shows that the more you wrap the wire around the nail, the more paper clips it picks up.

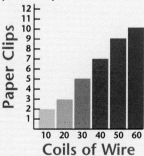

Coils of Wire

How many paper clips did the nail with 20 coils pick up? With 50 coils?

Line Graphs

A line graph shows information by connecting dots plotted on the graph. For example, what if you are growing a plant? Every week you measure how high the plant has grown. The line graph below organizes the measurements you collected so that you can easily compare them.

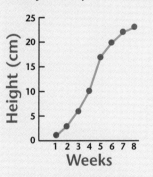

Weeks

1. Between which two weeks did the plant grow most?
2. When did plant growth begin to level off?

Make a Graph

What if you collect information about how much water your family uses each day?

Activity	Water Used (L)
Drinking	10
Showering	180
Bathing	240
Brushing teeth	80
Washing dishes	140
Washing hands	30
Washing clothes	280
Flushing toilet	90

Decide what type of graph would best organize such data. Collect the information and make your graph. Compare it with those of classmates.

Make Maps to Show Information

Locate Places

A map is a drawing that shows an area from above. Most maps have coordinates—numbers and letters along the top and side. Coordinates help you find places easily. For example, what if you wanted to find the library on the map? It is located at B4. Place a finger on the letter B along the side of the map, and another finger on the number 4 at the top. Then move your fingers straight across and down the map until they meet. The library is located where the coordinates B and 4 meet, or very nearby.

1. What color building is located at F6?
2. The hospital is located three blocks north and two blocks east of the library. What are its coordinates?
3. Make a map of an area in your community. It might be a park, or the area between your home and school. Include coordinates. Use a compass to find north, and mark north on your map. Exchange maps with classmates, and answer each other's questions.

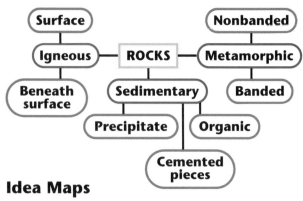

Idea Maps

The map shows how places are connected to each other. Idea maps, on the other hand, show how ideas are connected to each other. Idea maps help you organize information about a topic.

The idea map above connects ideas about rocks. This map shows that there are three major types of rock—igneous, sedimentary, and metamorphic. Connections to each rock type provide further information. For example, this map reminds you that igneous rocks are classified into those that form at Earth's surface and far beneath it.

Make an idea map about a topic you are learning in science. Your map can include words, phrases, or even sentences. Arrange your map in a way that makes sense to you and helps you understand the ideas.

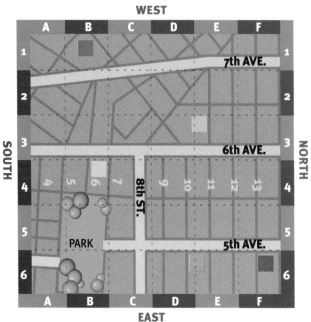

Make Tables and Charts to Organize Information

Tables help you organize data during experiments. Most tables have columns that run up and down, and rows that run across. The columns and rows have headings that tell you what kind of data goes in each part of the table.

A Sample Table

What if you are going to do an experiment to find out how long different kinds of seeds take to sprout? Before you begin the experiment, you should set up your table. Follow these steps.

1. In this experiment you will plant 20 radish seeds, 20 bean seeds, and 20 corn seeds. Your table must show how many radish seeds, bean seeds, and corn seeds sprouted on days 1, 2, 3, 4, and 5.

Make a Table

Now what if you are going to do an experiment to find out how temperature affects the sprouting of seeds? You will plant 20 bean seeds in each of two trays. You will keep each tray at a different temperature, as shown below, and observe the trays for seven days. Make a table you can use for this experiment.

Make a Chart

A chart is simply a table with pictures as well as words to label the rows or columns.

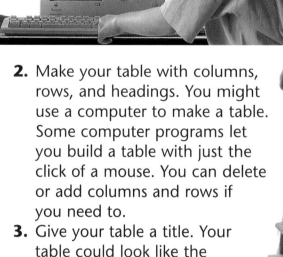

2. Make your table with columns, rows, and headings. You might use a computer to make a table. Some computer programs let you build a table with just the click of a mouse. You can delete or add columns and rows if you need to.

3. Give your table a title. Your table could look like the one here.

R23

Computer

A computer has many uses. The Internet connects your computer to many other computers around the world, so you can collect all kinds of information. You can use a computer to show this information and write reports. Best of all you can use a computer to explore, discover, and learn.

You can also get information from CD-ROMs. They are computer disks that can hold large amounts of information. You can fit a whole encyclopedia on one CD-ROM.

Use Computers for a Project

Here is how one group of students uses computers as they work on a weather project.

1. The students use instruments to measure temperature, wind speed, wind direction, and other parts of the weather. They input this information, or data, into the computer. The students keep the data in a table. This helps them compare the data from one day to the next.

2. The teacher finds out that another group of students in a town 200 kilometers to the west is also doing a weather project. The two groups use the Internet to talk to each other and share data. When a storm happens in the town to the west, that group tells the other group that it's coming their way.

3. The students want to find out more. They decide to stay on the Internet and send questions to a local TV weather forecaster. She has a Web site and answers questions from students every day.

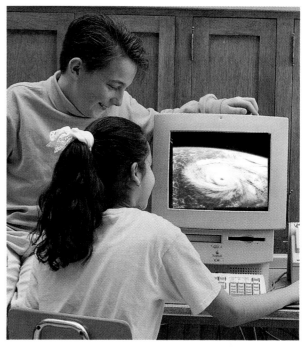

4. Meanwhile some students go to the library to gather more information from a CD-ROM disk. The CD-ROM has an encyclopedia that includes movie clips with sound. The clips give examples of different kinds of storms.

5. The students have kept all their information in a folder called Weather Project. Now they use that information to write a report about the weather. On the computer they can move around paragraphs, add words, take out words, put in diagrams, and draw their own weather maps. Then they print the report in color.

Calculator

Sometimes after you make measurements, you have to analyze your data to see what it means. This might involve doing calculations with your data. A calculator helps you do time-consuming calculations.

Find an Average

The table shows the lengths of a group of unshelled peanuts. What is the average length of the peanuts? You can use a calculator to help you find out.

Peanut	Length (mm)
1	32
2	29
3	30
4	31
5	33
6	26
7	28
8	27
9	29
10	29
11	32
12	31
13	23
14	36
15	31

1. Make sure the calculator is on. Press the [ON] key.
2. Add the numbers. To add a series of numbers, enter the first number and press [+]. Repeat until you enter the last number. Then press [=]. Your total should be 447.
3. While entering so many numbers, it's easy to make a mistake and hit the wrong key. If you make a mistake, you can correct it by pressing the clear entry key, [CE]. Then continue entering the rest of the numbers.
4. Look at the list of lengths, and estimate what you think the average length is. Find the average length of the peanuts by dividing your total by the number of peanuts. If 447 is displayed, press [÷][1][5][=]. How close was your estimate to the actual average?

GLOSSARY

This Glossary will help you to pronounce and understand the meanings of the Science Words introduced in this book. The page number at the end of the definition tells where the word appears.

A

abiotic factor (ā′bī ot′ik fak′tər) A nonliving part of an ecosystem. (p. 485)

absorption (əb sôrp′shən) The disappearance of a sound wave into a surface. (p. 220)

acid rain (as′id rān) Moisture that falls to Earth after being mixed with wastes from burned fossil fuels. (p. 449)

adaptation (ad′əp tā′shən) A characteristic that enables a living thing to survive in its environment. (pp. 86, 530)

aerial root (âr′ē əl rüt) A root that never touches the ground but can take in moisture from the air. (p. 20)

aerobic exercise (â rō′bik ek′sər sīz′) A brisk and constant physical activity that increases the supply of oxygen to the muscles. (p. 616)

aerosol (âr′ə sôl′) A type of colloid in which liquid drops or solid particles are spread throughout a gas. (p. 346)

air mass (âr mas) A large region of the atmosphere where the air has similar properties throughout. (p. 150)

air pressure (âr presh′ər) The force put on a given area by the weight of the air above it. (p. 105)

alternation of generations (ôl′tər nā′shən uv jen′ə rā′shənz) The process in which offspring are reproduced sexually, their offspring are reproduced asexually, and so on. (p. 49)

alternative energy source (ôl tûr′nə tiv en′ər jē sôrs) A source of energy other than the burning of a fossil fuel. (p. 472)

alveoli (al vē′ə lī′) n. pl., sing. **alveolus** (-ləs) Clusters of air sacs at the end of each bronchiole. (p. 593)

ammonia (ə mōn′yə) A simple substance that contains the element nitrogen. (p. 514)

anemometer (an′ə mom′i tər) A device that measures wind speed. (p. 142)

angiosperm (an′jē ə spûrm′) A seed plant that produces flowers. *See* **gymnosperm**. (p. 58)

antibody (an′ti bod′ē) A protein in blood that helps the body find and destroy materials that may be harmful. (p. 581)

antigen (an′ti jən) Either of two chemicals on the surfaces of type A or type B blood cells that limit their usefulness in providing blood transfusions. (p. 581)

aquifer (ak′wə fər) An underground layer of rock or soil filled with water. (p. 459)

artery (är′tə rē) A blood vessel that carries blood away from the heart. (p. 580)

asexual reproduction (a sek′shü əl rē′prō duk′shən) The production of a new organism from only one cell. (p. 50)

atmosphere (at′məs fîr′) The blanket of gases that surrounds Earth. (pp. 104, 395)

PRONUNCIATION KEY

The following symbols are used throughout the *McGraw-Hill Science* Glossaries.

a	**at**	e	**end**	o	**hot**	u	**up**	hw	**white**	ə about
ā	**ape**	ē	**me**	ō	**old**	ū	**use**	ng	**song**	taken
ä	**far**	i	**it**	ô	**fork**	ü	**rule**	th	**thin**	pencil
âr	**care**	ī	**ice**	oi	**oil**	u̇	**pull**	t͟h	**this**	lemon
		îr	**pierce**	ou	**out**	ûr	**turn**	zh	measure	circus

′ = *primary accent; shows which syllable takes the main stress, such as* **kil** *in* **kilogram** (kil′ə gram′)

′ = *secondary accent; shows which syllables take the lighter stresses, such as* **gram** *in* **kilogram**

atom (at'əm) The smallest unit of an element that retains the properties of that element. *See* **molecule**. (p. 312)

auditory nerve (ô'di tôr'e nûrv) The nerve that passes vibrations in the ear on to the brain, which interprets the vibrations as sound. (p. 199)

B

bacterium (bak tîr'ē əm) *sing., n., pl.* **bacteria** (-ē ə) A member of either of two kingdoms of one-celled living things that have no nucleus, or center, in their cell body. (p. 13)

balanced diet (bal'ənst dī'it) A diet, maintained over time, that includes a variety of foods providing nutrition in moderate amounts. (p. 618)

barometer (bə rom'i tər) A device for measuring air pressure. (p. 106)

Beaufort scale (bō'fərt skāl) A system for measuring wind speed by observing its effect on the surface of the sea, using a scale of 0 (low) to 12 (high) for each effect. (p. 143)

bench mark (bench märk) A plaque telling the exact location and elevation of a place. (p. 403)

benthos (ben'thos) Organisms that live on the bottom in aquatic ecosystems. (p. 552)

bile (bīl) A greenish-yellow fluid produced by the liver to digest fats. (p. 605)

bioluminescence (bī'o lü'mə nes'əns) Cool light produced by living organisms. (p. 237)

biomass (bī'ō mas') Plant matter or animal waste that can be used as a source of energy. (p. 474)

biome (bī'ōm) One of Earth's large ecosystems, with its own kind of climate, soil, plants, and animals. (p. 544)

biotic factor (bī ot'ik fak'tər) A living part of an ecosystem. (p. 484)

bladder (blad'ər) A muscular bag that collects urine produced by the kidneys. (p. 606)

boiling point (boil'ing point) The particular temperature for each substance at which it changes state from a liquid to a gas. (p. 325)

bronchial tubes (brong'kē əl tübz) The two tubes that connect the trachea to each of your lungs. (p. 593)

bronchioles (brong'kē olz) Smaller passages of the bronchial tubes that branch throughout the lungs. (p. 593)

buoyancy (boi'ən sē) The upward push of a liquid on an object placed in it. (p. 298)

C

cambium (kam'bē əm) The layer in plants that separates the xylem from the phloem. (p. 20)

camouflage (kam'ə fläzh') An animal's use of its appearance to protect itself against predators. (p. 89)

capillary (kap'ə ler'ē) The smallest type of blood vessel, where materials are exchanged between blood and body cells. (p. 580)

carbon cycle (kär'bən sī'kəl) The continuous exchange of carbon dioxide and oxygen among living things. (p. 516)

carbon dioxide (kär'bən dī ok'sīd) A compound needed by all living plants to make sugars. (p. 514)

carnivore (kär'nə vôr') An animal that eats another animal. (p. 500)

chemical change (kem'i kəl chānj) A change of matter that occurs when atoms link together in a new way, creating a new substance different from the original substances. (p. 356)

chemical reaction (kem'i kəl rē ak'shən) Another name for chemical change. (p. 356)

chlorofluorocarbons (CFCs) (klôr'ō flür'ō kär'bənz) Gases used in such things as refrigerators, freezers, and air conditioners. CFCs may make "holes" in the ozone layer. (p. 451)

chlorophyll (klôr'ə fil') A green chemical in plant cells that allows plants to use the Sun's energy for making food. (p. 4)

chloroplast (klôr'ə plast') The part of a plant cell containing chlorophyll, the green substance that enables the plant to produce food. (p. 32)

cilia (sil'ē ə) Small hairlike structures that move small particles of dirt out of the respiratory system. (p. 593)

cirrus cloud (sir'əs kloud) A high-altitude cloud with a featherlike shape, made of ice crystals. (p. 122)

classification (klas'ə fi kā'shən) The science of finding patterns among living things. (p. 5)

classify (klas′ə fī′) To place materials that share properties together in groups. (p. 301)

cleavage (klē′vij) The tendency of a mineral to break along flat surfaces. (p. 418)

climate (klī′mit) The average weather pattern of a region. (p. 178)

climatic zone (klī mat′ik zōn) A region that has similar weather patterns based on temperature, precipitation, wind, distance from a coast, mountain ranges, ocean currents, and vegetation. (p. 178)

climax community (klī′maks kə mū′ni tē) The final stage of succession in an area, unless a major change happens. (p. 564)

cold front (kōld frunt) A boundary where cold air moves in under a mass of warm air. (p. 152)

colloid (kol′oid) A special type of mixture in which the particles of one material are scattered through another and block the passage of light without settling out. (p. 346)

commensalism (kə men′sə liz′əm) A relationship between two kinds of organisms that benefits one without harming the other. (p. 535)

community (kə mū′ni tē) All the populations living in an area. (p. 488)

complete flower (kəm plēt′ flou′ər) A flower that has petals, stamens, and pistils. (p. 70)

compound (kom′pound) Any substance that is formed by the chemical combination of two or more elements and acts like a single substance. (p. 310)

compression (kəm presh′ən) 1. The part of a sound wave where molecules are crowded together. (p. 198) 2. A movement of plates that presses together or squeezes Earth's crust. (p. 404)

concave lens (kon kāv′ lenz) A lens that curves inward (is thicker at the edges than at the middle) and spreads light rays apart, making images appear smaller. (p. 254)

concave mirror (kon kav′ mir′ər) A mirror that curves in on the shiny side. (p. 242)

condensation (kon′den sā′shən) The changing of a gas into a liquid. (p. 115)

conduct (v., kən dukt′) To allow heat to pass through easily. (p. 300)

conduction (kən duk′shən) The passing of heat through a material while the material itself stays in place. (p. 375)

conifer (kon′ə fər) Any of a group of gymnosperms that produce seeds in cones and have needlelike leaves. (p. 59)

consumer (kən sü′mər) Any animal that eats plants or eats other plant-eating animals. (p. 485)

contour plowing (kon′tür plou′ing) Preventing erosion by plowing across rather than up and down a slope. (p. 437)

contract (v., kən trakt′) To shrink, as when a material gets cooler. (p. 331)

convection (kən vek′shən) The flow of heat through a material, causing hot parts to rise and cooler parts to sink. (p. 375)

convection cell (kən vek′shən sel) A circular pattern of air rising, air sinking, and wind. (p. 136)

convex lens (kon veks′ lenz) A lens that curves outward (is thicker at the middle than at the edges) and brings light together, making images appear larger. (p. 254)

convex mirror (kon veks′ mir′ər) A mirror that curves out on the shiny side. (p. 242)

core (kôr) The center of Earth, lying below the mantle. (p. 403)

Coriolis effect (kôr′ē ō′lis i fekt′) The curving of the path of a moving object caused by Earth's rotation. (p. 138)

cortex (kôr′teks) The layer of tissue just inside the epidermis of a plant's roots and stems. (p. 20)

cotyledon (ko′tə lē′dən) A tiny leaflike structure inside the seed of an angiosperm. (p. 62)

PRONUNCIATION KEY

a at; ā ape; ä far; âr care; e end; ē me; i it; ī ice; îr pierce; o hot; ō old; ô fork; oi oil; ou out; u up; ū use; ü rule; ů pull; ûr turn; hw white; ng song; th thin; th this; zh measure; ə about, taken, pencil, lemon, circus

GLOSSARY

crop rotation (krop rō tā'shən) Growing different crops each year so that the soil does not use up the same kinds of minerals year after year. (p. 437)

cross-pollination (krôs'pol'ə nā'shən) The transfer of pollen from one flower to another. (p. 72)

crust (krust) The rocky surface that makes up the top of the lithosphere and includes the continents and the ocean floor. (p. 394)

crystal (kris'təl) The geometric shape a mineral forms when its atoms and molecules get into fixed patterns. (p. 416)

cumulus cloud (kū'myə ləs kloud) A puffy cloud that appears to rise up from a flat bottom. (p. 122)

cycad (sī'kad) One of the evergreen gymnosperms that resemble palms and have seed-bearing cones. (p. 59)

D

decibel (dB) (des'ə bel') A unit that measures loudness. (p. 210)

deciduous (di sij'ü əs) Said of a plant that loses its leaves each fall. *See* **evergreen**. (p. 59)

deciduous forest (di sij'ü əs fôr'ist) A forest biome with many kinds of trees that lose their leaves each autumn. (p. 550)

decomposer (dē'kəm pō'zər) Any of the fungi or bacteria that break down dead plants and animals into useful things like minerals and rich soil. (p. 485)

density (den'si tē) A measure of how tightly packed the matter in an object is. (p. 295)

deposition (dep'ə zish'ən) The dropping off of bits of eroded rock. (p. 409)

desalination (dē sal'ə nā'shən) Getting fresh water from seawater. (p. 457)

desert (dez'ərt) A sandy or rocky biome with little precipitation and little plant life. (p. 549)

diaphragm (dī'ə fram') A sheet of muscle below the chest cavity that controls breathing. (p. 592)

dicot (dī'kot') An angiosperm with two cotyledons in each seed. *See* **monocot**. (p. 62)

diffusion (di fū'zhən) The process by which a substance such as a gas moves from areas of high concentration to areas of low concentration. (p. 593)

digestion (di jes'chən) The process of breaking food down into simpler substances for the body to use. (p. 604)

Doppler effect (dop'lər i fekt') The change in frequency (and pitch) as a source of sound moves toward or away from you. (p. 225)

downdraft (doun'draft') A downward rush of air caused by the falling of rain during a thunderstorm. (p. 162)

dry cell battery (drī sel bat'ər ē) A battery that produces electricity but has no liquid inside it. (p. 379)

E

echo (e'kō) A reflected sound wave. (p. 222)

echolocation (ek'ō lō kā'shən) Finding an object by using reflected sound. (p. 224)

ecological succession (ek'ə loj'i kəl sək sesh'ən) The gradual replacement of one community by another. (p. 562)

ecology (ē kol'ə jē) The study of how living things and their environment interact. (p. 484)

ecosystem (ek'ō sis'təm) All the living and nonliving things in an area and their interactions with each other. (p. 484)

electromagnetic spectrum (i lek'trō mag net'ik spek'trəm) All the wavelengths of visible and invisible light in order, from short (gamma rays) to long (radio). (p. 277)

electromagnetism (i lek'trō mag'ni tiz'əm) The production of magnetism by electricity (and the production of electricity by magnets). (p. 276)

electron (i lek'tron) A particle in the space outside the nucleus of an atom that carries one unit of negative electric charge. (p. 313)

element (el'ə mənt) Pure substances that cannot be broken down into any simpler substances. (p. 308)

elevation (el'ə vā'shən) How high a place is above sea level. (p. 403)

embryo (em'brē ō') The immature plant inside a seed. (p. 74)

emulsion (i mul′shən) A type of colloid in which one liquid is spread through another. (p. 346)

enzyme (en′zīm) A substance in a living thing that affects how fast chemical reactions take place. (p. 604)

epidermis (ep′i dûr′mis) An outermost layer of such plant parts as roots and leaves. (p. 20)

epiglottis (ep′i glot′is) A cartilage flap above the trachea that keeps food from entering the lungs. (p. 593)

erosion (i rō′zhən) Picking up and carrying away pieces of rocks. (p. 407)

esophagus (i sof′ə gəs) The tube that connects the mouth to the stomach. (p. 604)

evaporation (i vap′ə rā′shən) The changing of a liquid into a gas. (pp. 112, 325)

evergreen (ev′ər grēn′) Seed of a gymnosperm that keeps its leaves for at least a few years. *See* **deciduous**. (p. 59)

excretion (ek skrē′shən) The process of removing waste products from the body. (p. 606)

expand (ek spand′) To spread out, as when a material gets hotter. (p. 331)

F

fault (fôlt) A crack in the crust whose sides show evidence of motion. (p. 402)

fault-block mountain (fôlt blok moun′tən) A mountain formed by blocks of Earth′s crust moving along a fault. (p. 405)

fertilization (fûr′tə lə zā′shən) The joining of a female sex cell and a male sex cell into one cell, a fertilized egg. (pp. 50, 73)

fertilizer (fûr′tə līz′ər) Nitrogen-containing substances used to make soil better for growing plants. (p. 515)

fibrous root (fī′brəs rüt) One of the many hairy branching roots that some plants have. (p. 20)

foam (fōm) A type of colloid in which a gas is spread throughout a liquid. (p. 347)

fog (fôg) A cloud that forms at ground level. (p. 123)

food chain (füd chān) The path of the energy in food from one organism to another. (p. 498)

food cycle (füd sī′kəl) The continual reuse of substances needed to survive as they are passed along from one organism to the next. (p. 514)

food group (füd grüp) One of the groups made up of foods that contain similar amounts of important nutrients. (p. 618)

food web (füd web) The overlapping food chains in an ecosystem. (p. 500)

fossil (fos′əl) Any remains or imprint of living things of the past. (p. 431)

fossil fuel (fos′əl fū′əl) A fuel formed from the decay of ancient forms of life. (p. 448)

freezing point (frēz′ing point) Another name for melting point when a substance changes state from a liquid to a solid. (p. 325)

frequency (frē′kwən sē) The number of times an object vibrates per second. (p. 209)

frond (frond) The leaf of a fern. (p. 49)

front (frunt) A boundary between air masses with different temperatures. (p. 151)

fruit (früt) The ripened ovary of a flowering seed plant. (p. 75)

fundamental frequency (fun′də men′təl frē′kwən sē) The lowest frequency at which an object vibrates. (p. 226)

fungi (fun′jī) *pl. n., sing.* **fungus** (fung′gəs) Members of a kingdom that contains one-celled and many-celled living things that absorb food from their environment. (p. 11)

G

gel (jel) A type of colloid in which a solid is spread throughout a liquid. (p. 347)

gem (jem) A mineral valued for being rare and beautiful. (p. 422)

PRONUNCIATION KEY

a **a**t; ā **a**pe; ä f**a**r; âr c**a**re; e **e**nd; ē m**e**; i **i**t; ī **i**ce; îr p**i**erce; o h**o**t; ō **o**ld; ô f**o**rk; oi **oi**l; ou **ou**t; u **u**p; ū **u**se;
ü r**u**le; ù p**u**ll; ûr t**u**rn; hw **wh**ite; ng so**ng**; th **th**in; <u>th</u> **th**is; zh mea**s**ure; ə **a**bout, tak**e**n, penc**i**l, lem**o**n, circ**u**s

geologist (jē ol'ə jist) A scientist who studies Earth. (p. 403)

geothermal energy (jē'ō thûr'məl en'ər jē) Earth's internal energy. (p. 472)

germination (jûr'mə nā'shən) The sprouting of a seed into a new plant. (p. 75)

ginkgo (ging'kō) *n., pl.* **ginkgoes** A large gymnosperm with fan-shaped leaves. (p. 59)

gnetophyte (ne'tō fīt') One of the gymnosperms that are closely related to flowering plants and live in both deserts and the tropics. (p. 59)

grassland (gras'land') A biome where grasses, not trees, are the main plant life. Prairies are one kind of grassland region. (p. 546)

gravitropism (grav'i trō'pi'zəm) The response of a plant to gravity. (p. 84)

gravity (grav'i tē) A force of attraction, or pull, between any object and any other objects around it. Gravity is a property of all matter. (p. 390)

greenhouse effect (grēn'hous' i fekt') The ability of the atmosphere to let in sunlight but not to let heat escape. (p. 183)

groundwater (ground wô'tər) Water that seeps into the ground into spaces between bits of rock and soil. (pp. 126, 459)

gymnosperm (jim'nə spûrm') A seed plant that does not produce flowers. *See* **angiosperm**. (p. 58)

H

habitat (hab'i tat') The area in which an organism lives. (p. 489)

hail (hāl) Pellets made of ice and snow. (p. 125)

hardness (härd'nis) How well a mineral resists scratching. (p. 418)

hemoglobin (hē'mə glō'bin) A chemical that carries oxygen around in the body. (p. 580)

herbivore (hûr'bə vôr') An animal that eats plants, algae, and other producers. (p. 500)

hertz (Hz) (hûrts) A unit for measuring frequency. One hertz (Hz) equals a frequency of one vibration per second. (p. 209)

high-pressure system (hī' presh'ər sis'təm) A pattern surrounding a high-pressure center, from which winds blow outward. In the Northern Hemisphere, these winds curve to the right in a clockwise pattern. (p. 140)

humidity (hū mid'i tē) The amount of water vapor in the air. (p. 112)

humus (hū'məs) Decayed plant or animal material in soil. (p. 435)

hurricane (hûr'i kān') A very large, swirling storm with very low pressure at the center. (p. 166)

hydrocarbon (hī'drə kär'bən) Any of the large group of compounds made solely from hydrogen and carbon atoms. (p. 318)

hydroelectric plant (hī'drō i lek'trik plant) A factory where running or falling water spins a generator to make electricity. (p. 472)

hydrosphere (hī'drə sfîr') Earth's water, whether found in continents and oceans, and includes the fresh water in ice, lakes, rivers, and underground water. (p. 394)

hydrotropism (hī drot'rə piz'əm) The response of a plant to a nearby source of water. (p. 85)

hyperthermia (hī'pər thûr'mē ə) The overheating of the body that can be caused by overexposure in a hot, dry climate. (p. 186)

hypothesis (hī poth'ə sis) A guess or *if . . . then* statement that can be answered clearly in an experiment. (p. 35)

I-K

igneous rock (ig'nē əs rok) A rock formed when melted rock material cools and hardens. (p. 428)

image (im'ij) A "picture" of the light source that light rays make in bouncing off a polished, shiny surface. (p. 242)

imperfect flower (im pûr'fikt flou'ər) A flower with either a stamen or a pistil, but not both. (p. 70)

incomplete flower (in'kəm plēt' flou'ər) A flower that lacks petals or stamens or pistils. (p. 70)

inertia (i nûr'shə) The tendency of a moving object to keep moving in a straight line. (p. 391)

insolation (in'sə lā'shən) The amount of the Sun's energy that reaches Earth at a given time and place. *Insolation* is short for *in*coming *sol*ar *radi*ation. (p. 100)

insulate (in'sə lāt') To prevent heat from passing through. (p. 300)

intertidal zone (in'tər tī'dəl zōn) The shallowest section of the marine, or ocean, ecosystem, where the ocean floor is covered and uncovered as the tide goes in and out. (p. 553)

isobar (i'sə bär') A line on a weather map connecting places with equal air pressure. (p. 140)

kinetic energy (ki net'ik en'ər jē) The energy of any moving object. (p. 369)

L

land breeze (land brēz) Wind that blows from land to sea. (p. 137)

larynx (lar'ingks) The voice box, located at the upper end of the trachea. (p. 593)

laser (lā'zər) A device that produces a thin stream of light of just a few close wavelengths. (p. 282)

lava (lä'və) Magma that reaches Earth's surface. (p. 405)

law of reflection (lô uv ri flek'shən) The angle between an incoming light ray and a surface equals the angle between the reflected light ray and the surface. (p. 241)

lightning (līt'ning) One of the huge electric sparks that leap from clouds to the ground in thunderstorms. (p. 162)

light ray (līt rā) A straight-line beam of light as it travels outward from its source. (p. 239)

limiting factor (lim'ə ting fak'tər) Anything that controls the growth or survival of a population. (p. 528)

lithosphere (lith'ə sfîr') The hard, outer layer of Earth, about 100 kilometers thick. (p. 394)

long-day plant (lông'dā plant) Plants that bloom when there is much more daylight than darkness. (p. 86)

low-pressure system (lō'presh'ər sis'təm) A pattern surrounding a low-pressure center, in which winds blow in toward the center. In the Northern Hemisphere, these winds blow to the right in a counterclockwise pattern. (p. 140)

luster (lus'tər) The way light bounces off a mineral's surface. (p. 417)

M

magma (mag'mə) Hot, molten rock deep below Earth's surface. (p. 405)

mantle (man'təl) The thickest layer of Earth, lying just under the crust. (p. 403)

mass (mas) A measure of the amount of matter in an object. (p. 292)

matter (ma'tər) Anything that has mass and takes up space. (p. 198)

melting point (melt'ing point) The particular temperature for each substance at which it changes state from a solid to a liquid. (p. 325)

membrane (mem'brān) A thin envelope surrounding the nucleus of a cell. (p. 12)

metamorphic rock (met'ə môr'fik rok) A rock formed under heat and pressure from another kind of rock. (p. 432)

meteorite (mē'tē ə rīt') A chunk of rock from space that strikes a surface (such as Earth or the Moon). (p. 410)

mimicry (mim'i krē) An animal's use of its appearance to look like a different, unpleasant animal as a protection against predators. (p. 89)

mineral (min'ər əl) A solid material of Earth's crust with a definite composition. (p. 416)

mixture (miks'chər) A physical combination of two or more substances that are blended together without forming new substances. (p. 340)

molecule (mol'ə kūl') The smallest piece that matter can be broken into without changing the kind of matter; a group of more than one atom joined together that acts like a single particle. *See* **atom**. (pp. 198, 316)

PRONUNCIATION KEY

a **at**; ā **ape**; ä **far**; âr **care**; e **end**; ē **me**; i **it**; ī **ice**; îr **pierce**; o **hot**; ō **old**; ô **fork**, oi **oil**; ou **out**; u **up**; ū **use**; u **rule**; u̇ **pull**; ûr **turn**; hw **white**; ng **song**; th **thin**; <u>th</u> **this**; zh **measure**; ə **about, taken, pencil, lemon, circus**

GLOSSARY

monocot (mon′ə kot′) An angiosperm with one cotyledon in each seed. *See* **dicot**. (p. 62)

mountain breeze (moun′tən brēz) A cool night wind that blows down a mountain slope to replace the warmer air in the valley. (p. 137)

mucus (mū′kəs) A sticky fluid that traps and prevents foreign particles from entering the body. (p. 593)

mutualism (mū′chü ə liz′əm) A relationship between two kinds of organisms that benefits both. (p. 532)

N

nekton (nek′ton) Organisms that swim through the water in aquatic ecosystems. (p. 552)

nephron (nef′ron) A structure in the kidney that filters blood. (p. 606)

neutron (nü′tron) A particle in the nucleus of an atom that has no net electric charge. (p. 313)

NEXRAD (neks′rad′) A new form of Doppler radar that is used to track storms. The word stands for *NEXt generation of weather RADar.* (p. 173)

niche (nich) The role an organism has in its ecosystem. (p. 489)

nitrogen (nī′trə jən) An element that plants need to grow and stay healthy, and that all organisms need to make proteins. (p. 515)

nitrogen cycle (nī′trə jən sī′kəl) The continuous trapping of nitrogen gas into compounds in the soil and its return to the air. (p. 518)

nonrenewable resource (non′ri nü′ə bəl rē′sôrs′) A resource that cannot be replaced within a short period of time or at all. (p. 423)

nonvascular (non vas′kyə lər) Containing no plant tissue through which water and food move. (p. 7)

nucleus (nü′klē əs) 1. A dense, dark structure inside the cell. (p. 12) 2. One of the airborne dust particles around which water molecules condense as droplets or ice crystals before falling as precipitation. (p. 123)

O

occluded front (ə klüd′id frunt) A front formed where a cold front moves in under a warm front. (p. 152)

omnivore (om′nə vôr′) An animal that eats both plants and animals. (p. 501)

opaque (ō pāk′) Completely blocking light from passing through it. (p. 250)

orbit (ôr′bit) The path of a planet traveling around a star. (p. 388)

ore (ôr) A mineral containing a useful substance. (p. 422)

ovary (ō′və rē) A structure containing egg cells. (p. 72)

overtone (ō′vər tōn′) One of a series of pitches that blend to give a sound its quality. (p. 226)

ozone layer (ō′zōn lā′ər) A layer of ozone gas in the atmosphere that screens out much of the Sun's UV (ultraviolet) rays. (p. 447)

P

parasite (par′ə sīt′) An angiosperm that lives off other plants. It cannot live on its own because it has little or no chlorophyll. (p. 60)

parasitism (par′ə sī tiz′əm) A relationship in which one kind of organism lives on and may harm another. (p. 534)

perfect flower (pûr′fikt flou′ər) A flower with both male and female parts, that is, both a stamen and a pistil. (p. 70)

periodic table (pîr′ē od′ik tā′bəl) A table in which the elements are arranged in groups with similar properties. (p. 315)

phloem (flō′em) The tissue through which food from the leaves moves down through the rest of a plant. (p. 20)

photon (fō′ton) The tiny bundles of energy by means of which light travels. (p. 277)

photoperiodism (fō′tō pîr′ē ə diz′əm) The flowering response of a plant to changing periods of daylight and darkness. (p. 86)

photosynthesis (fō′tə sin′thə sis) The food-making process in green plants that uses sunlight. (p. 32)

phototropism (fō tot′rə piz′əm) The response of a plant to changes in light. (p. 84)

phylum (fī′ləm) *sing. n., pl.* **phyla** (-lə) One of the large groups in the animal kingdom. (p. 10)

physical change (fiz'i kəl chānj) A change of matter in size, shape, or state without any change in identity. (p. 354)

physical fitness (fiz'i kəl fit'nis) The condition in which your body is healthy and works the best it can. (p. 616)

pioneer community (pī'ə nîr' kə mū'ni tē) The first community thriving in a once lifeless area. (p. 564)

pioneer species (pī'ə nîr' spē'shēz) The first species living in an otherwise lifeless area. (p. 563)

pitch (pich) How high or low a sound is. (p. 208)

planet (plan'it) Any of the nine large bodies that travel around the Sun and shine by reflecting its light. (p. 388)

plankton (plangk'tən) Organisms that float on the water in aquatic ecosystems. (p. 552)

plant behavior (plant bi hāv'yər) The response of plants to conditions in their environments. (p. 82)

plasma (plaz'mə) The pale-yellow liquid part of blood that contains nutrients. (p. 580)

plate (plāt) One of the pieces of Earth's crust that has been broken by upward pressure from the mantle. (p. 403)

platelet (plāt'lit) A cell fragment in blood that helps blood to form clots. (p. 580)

polarization (pō'lər ə zā'shən) Allowing light vibrations to pass through in only one direction. (p. 251)

pollen (pol'ən) Dustlike grains in the flower of a plant that contain its male sex cells. (p. 64)

pollination (pol'ə nā'shən) The transfer of a pollen grain to the egg-producing part of a plant. (p. 72)

pollutant (pə lü'tənt) An unnatural substance added to Earth's land, water, or air. (p. 436)

pollution (pə lü'shən) Adding any harmful substances to Earth's land, water, or air. (p. 436)

polymer (pol'ə mər) Any plastic, such as polyethylene, that is made of hydrocarbon molecules with very long chains of atoms. (p. 318)

population (pop'yə lā'shən) All the members of one species in an area. (p. 488)

potential energy (pə ten'shəl en'ər jē) Stored energy. (p. 369)

precipitation (pri sip'i tā'shən) Any form of water particles that falls from the atmosphere and reaches the ground. (p. 124)

predator (pred'ə tər) A living thing that hunts other living things for food. (p. 501)

prey (prā) A living thing that is hunted for food. (p. 501)

primary color (prī'mer'ē kul'ər) Red, green, or blue. Mixing these colors can produce all the colors of the spectrum. (p. 266)

primary pigment (prī'mer'ē pig'mənt) Magenta, cyan, or yellow. Materials with any of these colors absorb one primary color of light and reflect the other two. (p. 268)

prism (priz'əm) A cut piece of clear glass (or plastic) with two opposite sides in the shape of a triangle or other geometric shape. (p. 264)

producer (prə dü'sər) Any of the plants and algae that produce oxygen and food that animals need. (p. 485)

product (prod'ukt) A new substance produced by a chemical change. (p. 356)

property (prop'ər tē) A characteristic of matter. (p. 292)

prop root (prop rüt) One of the roots that grow out of a plant's stemlike main roots and helps prop up the plant. (p. 20)

protective coloration (prə tek'tiv kul'ə rā'shən) An animal's blending in with its background to protect itself against predators. (p. 89)

protist (prō'tist) A member of a kingdom that contains one-celled and many-celled living things, some that make food and some that hunt for food. (p. 12)

GLOSSARY

PRONUNCIATION KEY

a at; ā ape; ä far; âr care; e end; ē me; i it; ī ice; îr pierce; o hot; ō old; ô fork; oi oil; ou out; u up; ū use; ü rule; ù pull; ûr turn; hw white; ng song; th thin; <u>th</u> this; zh measure; ə about, taken, pencil, lemon, circus

proton (prō′ton) A particle in the nucleus of an atom that carries one unit of positive electric charge. (p. 313)

Q-R

quality (kwol′i tē) The difference you hear between two sounds of the same loudness and pitch. (p. 226)

radiation (rā′dē a′shən) The giving off of infrared rays through space. (p. 375)

radiative balance (rā′dē ā′tiv bal′əns) A balance between energy lost and energy gained. (p. 182)

rarefaction (râr′ə fak′shən) The part of a sound wave where molecules are spread apart. (p. 198)

reactant (rē ak′tənt) An original substance at the beginning of a chemical reaction. (p. 356)

reflection (ri flek′shən) The bouncing of a sound wave off a surface. (p. 220)

refraction (ri frak′shən) The bending of light rays as they pass from one substance into another. (p. 252)

relative humidity (rel′ə tiv hū mid′i tē) A comparison between condensation and evaporation. (p. 114)

renewable resource (ri nü′ə bəl rē′sôrs′) A resource that can be replaced in a short period of time. (p. 446)

reservoir (rez′ər vwär′) A storage area for freshwater supplies. (p. 459)

resource (rē′sôrs′) Any material that helps support life on Earth. (p. 386)

respiration (res′pə rā′shən) **1.** The process of obtaining and using oxygen in the body. (p. 592) **2.** The release of energy in plants from food (sugar). (p. 33)

response (ri spons′) What a living thing does as a result of a stimulus. (p. 84)

rhizoid (rī′zoid) One of the hairlike fibers that anchors a moss to the soil and takes in water from the soil. (p. 46)

rhizome (rī′zōm) The underground stem of a fern. (p. 49)

rock (rok) A naturally formed solid in the crust made up of one or more minerals. (p. 428)

rock cycle (rok sī′kəl) Rocks changing from one form into another in a never-ending series of processes. (p. 438)

root cap (rüt kap) A thin covering made up of cells that protect the root tip of a plant as it grows into the soil. (p. 20)

runoff (run′ôf) Precipitation that falls into rivers and streams. (p. 126)

S

scavenger (skav′ən jər) A meat-eating animal that feeds on the remains of dead animals. (p. 501)

sea breeze (sē brēz) Wind that blows from sea to land. (p. 137)

sedimentary rock (sed′ə men′tə rē rok) A rock made of bits of matter joined together. (p. 430)

seed (sēd) An undeveloped plant with stored food sealed in a protective covering. (p. 58)

seed coat (sēd kōt) The outer covering of a seed. (p. 74)

seed dispersal (sēd di spûr′səl) The movement of a seed from the flower to a place where it can sprout. (p. 75)

self-pollination (self′pol′ə nā′shən) The transfer of pollen from an anther to a stigma in the same plant. (p. 72)

sexual reproduction (sek′shü əl rē′prō duk′shən) The production of a new organism from a female sex cell and a male sex cell. (p. 50)

shear (shîr) A movement of plates that twists, tears, or pushes one part of Earth's crust past another. (p. 404)

short-day plant (shôrt′dā plant) Plants that bloom when there is more darkness and less daylight. (p. 86)

sickle cell anemia (sik′əl sel ə nē′mē ə) An inherited blood disease in which the red blood cells curve into a C shape and cannot move or absorb oxygen easily. (p. 586)

smog (smog) A mixture of smoke and fog. (p. 448)

solar system (sō′lər sis′təm) The Sun and the objects that are traveling around it. (p. 388)

solution (sə lü'shən) A mixture of substances that are blended so completely that the mixture looks the same everywhere, even under a microscope. (p. 344)

sound wave (sound wāv) A vibration that spreads away from a vibrating object. (p. 198)

spectrum (spek'trəm) A band of colors produced when light goes through a prism. (p. 264)

spore (spôr) A cell in a seedless plant that grows into a new organism. (p. 46)

spring (spring) A place where groundwater seeps out of the ground. (p. 459)

states of matter (stāts uv mat'ər) One of the three forms that matter can take—solid, liquid, or gas. (p. 324)

stationary front (stā'shə ner ē frunt) An unmoving front where a cold air mass and a warm air mass meet. (p. 153)

statistical forecasting (stə tis'ti kəl fôr'kas'ting) Predicting weather by using past weather records, based on the chances of a pattern repeating itself. (p. 156)

stimulus (stim'yə ləs), *sing., pl.* **stimuli** (-lī) Something in the environment that causes a living thing to react. (p. 84)

stomata (stō'mə tə) *pl. n., sing.* **stoma** Pores in the bottom of leaves that open and close to let in air or give off water vapor. (p. 25)

storm surge (stôrm sûrj) A great rise of the sea along a shore caused by low-pressure clouds. (p. 168)

stratus cloud (strā'təs kloud) A cloud that forms in a blanketlike layer. (p. 122)

streak (strēk) The color of the powder left when a mineral is rubbed against a hard, rough surface. (p. 418)

strip farming (strip fär'ming) Trapping runoff by alternating tightly growing grasses with more widely spaced plants. (p. 437)

surveyor (sər vā'ər) A specialist who makes accurate measurements of Earth's crust. (p. 403)

suspension (sə spen'shən) Mixtures in which suspended particles can easily be seen. (p. 345)

symbiosis (sim'bi ō'sis) A relationship between two kinds of organisms over time. (p. 532)

synoptic weather map (si nop'tik weth'ər map) A type of map showing a summary of the weather using station models. (p. 156)

T

taiga (tī'gə) A cool, forest biome of conifers in the upper Northern Hemisphere. (p. 547)

taproot (tap'rüt') A root that has few hairy branches and grows deep into the ground. (p. 20)

tension (ten'shən) A movement of plates that stretches or pulls apart Earth's crust. (p. 404)

terracing (ter'is ing) Shaping hillsides into steps so that runoff and eroded soil get trapped on the steps. (p. 437)

thunder (thun'dər) The noise caused by lightning-heated air during a thunderstorm. (p. 162)

thunderhead (thun'dər hed') A cumulonimbus cloud in which a thunderstorm forms. (p. 162)

thunderstorm (thun'dər stôrm') The most common severe storm, formed in cumulonimbus clouds. (p. 162)

tidal power plant (tī'dəl pou'ər plant) A factory where the flow of tidewater is used to make electricity. (p. 473)

tissue (tish'ü) A group of similar cells that work together at the same job. (p. 5)

tornado (tôr nā'dō) A violent whirling wind that moves across the ground in a narrow path. (p. 164)

trachea (trā'kē ə) A stiff tube lined with cartilage that transports air between the throat and lungs. (p. 593)

trade winds (trād windz) A belt of winds around Earth moving from high pressure zones toward the low pressure at the equator. (p. 139)

PRONUNCIATION KEY
a at; ā ape; ä far; âr care; e end; ē me; i it; ī ice; îr pierce; o hot; ō old; ô fork; oi oil; ou out; u up; ū use; ü rule; ú pull; ûr turn; hw white; ng song; th thin; th this; zh measure; ə about, taken, pencil, lemon, circus

transfusion (trans fū′zhən) Taking blood from one person and giving it to another person. (p. 581)

translucent (trans lü′sənt) Letting only some light through, so that objects on the other side appear blurry. (p. 250)

transparent (trans pâr′ənt) Letting all light through, so that objects on the other side can be seen clearly. (p. 250)

transpiration (tran′spə rā′shən) The loss of water through a plant's leaves, which draws water up through the plant to replace it. (pp. 25, 113)

tropical rain forest (trop′i kəl rān fôr′ist) A hot, humid biome near the equator, with much rainfall and a wide variety of life. (p. 551)

tropism (trō′piz′əm) A growth response of a plant toward or away from a stimulus. (p. 84)

troposphere (trop′ə sfîr′) The layer of the atmosphere closest to Earth's surface. (p. 104)

tundra (tun′drə) A cold, treeless biome of the far north, marked by spongy topsoil. (p. 548)

U

ultrasonic (ul′trə son′ik) Said of a sound with a frequency too high to be heard by humans. (p. 209)

updraft (up′draft′) An upward rush of heated air during a thunderstorm. (p. 162)

urea (yu̇ rē′ə) A substance formed from waste material in the liver and excreted in urine. (p. 606)

ureter (yu̇ rē′tər) One of two long, narrow tubes that carry urine from the kidneys to the bladder. (p. 606)

urethra (yu̇ rē′thrə) The tube through which urine passes from the body. (p. 606)

V

vacuum (vak′ū əm) A space through which sound waves cannot travel because it contains no matter. (p. 274)

valley breeze (val′ē brēz) A cool wind that blows up a mountain slope and replaces the slope's rising Sun-warmed air. (p. 137)

variable (vâr′ē ə bəl) One of the changes in a situation that may affect the outcome of an experiment. (p. 35)

vascular (vas′kyə lər) Containing plant tissue through which water moves up and food moves down. (p. 7)

vein (vān) A blood vessel that carries blood toward the heart. (p. 580)

vibration (vī brā′shən) A back-and-forth motion. (p. 196)

villus (vil′əs) *n., pl.* **villi** (vil′ī) One of many tiny fingerlike projections in the small intestine that absorb digested food. (p. 605)

volume (vol′ūm) A measure of how much space an object takes up. (p. 292)

W-X

warm front (wôrm frunt) A boundary where warm air moves in over a mass of cold air. (p. 152)

water cycle (wô′tər sī′kəl) The continuous movement of water between Earth's surface and the air, changing from liquid to gas to liquid. (pp. 127, 458, 512)

waterspout (wô′tər spout′) A tornado that forms over water. (p. 165)

water table (wô′tər tā′bəl) The top of the water-filled spaces in the ground. (p. 459)

water vapor (wô′tər vā′pər) Water in the form of a gas. (p. 112)

weather (weth′ər) What the lower atmosphere is like at any given place and time. (p. 106)

weathering (weth′ər ing) Breaking down rocks into smaller pieces. (p. 407)

weight (wāt) The force of gravity between Earth and an object. (p. 293)

well (wel) A hole dug below the water table that water seeps into. (p. 459)

wet cell battery (wet sel bat′ə rē) A battery that uses a chemical solution to produce electricity. (p. 378)

wind (wind) Air that moves horizontally. (p. 136)

wind vane (wind vān) A device that indicates wind direction. (p. 142)

xylem (zī′ləm) The tissue through which water and minerals move up through a plant. (p. 20)

INDEX

*Indicates an activity related to this topic.

X

*Indicates an activity related to this topic.

CREDITS

Maps: Geosystems

Transvision: Richard Hutchings (photography, TP1); Guy Porfirio (illustration)

Illustrations: Denny Bond: pp. 33, 518; Ka Botzis: pp. 500-501, 598, 612-613; Dan Clifford: p. 512; Barbara Cousins: pp. 239, 242-244, 254, 299, 580, 582-583, 605, 608, 618; Marie Dauenheimer: pp. 4, 5; Drew-Brook-Cormack: pp. 116, 123; John Edwards: pp. 224, 239, 242-244, 254, 293, 296, 299, 388; Peter Fasolino: pp. 333, 346; Robert Frank: pp. 516, 536; Thomas Gagliano: pp. 134-135, 137; Greg Harris: pp. 151, 181, 553; Virge Kask: pp. 10, 70, 72-74, 76-77, 498, 504-505; George Kelvin: pp. 24, 32, 35, 50-52, 83, 85-86, 93, 276, 394, 403-404, 409, 433, 435, 446-447, 458-459, 470; Katie Lee: pp. 32, 54, 484-485, 560-561, 564; Tom Leonard: pp. 199, 256-257; Rebecca Merrilees: pp. 20-23, 37-38, 49; Dave Merrill: pp. 395, 405, 487, 531-532; Mowry Graphics: pp. 126, 150, 185, 553; Steve Oh: pp. 585, 592, 593, 604, 606; Saul Rosenbaum: pp. 96, 102-103, 114, 125, 136, 152, 162-163, 165, 183, 253, 274-275; Wendy Smith: pp. 6, 8-9, 60, 62, 268; Steve Stankiewicz: pp. 114, 138, 148-149, 156, 161, 165, 169, 174, 185, 228, 235, 240, 247, 255, 260, 261, 266, 270-271, 282, 284, 326, 332, 334, 342, 350, 368, 371, 373, 378-380, 416-417, 438, 457, 462, 468, 544, 556, 569, R13, R15, R18-R20; Art Thompson: pp. 100, 140, 166, 178, 180, 188, 295, 299, 341-343, 348, 392-393.

Photography Credits: All photographs are by Richard Hutchings Photography except as noted below:

iii: images copyright ©1998 PhotoDisc, Inc. iv: NASA/Digital Stock. v: Digital Stock. vi: ©Cabisco/VU. vii: NASA/Digital Stock. viii: ©John D. Cunningham/VU. ix: Ken Eward/Science Source/Photo Researchers, Inc. S2, S3: ©David M. Sanders; S4: *t.r.* J.A. Kraulis/Masterfile; *b.r.* Antman/The Image Works; *bkmk.* Tom & Pat Leeson/Photo Researchers, Inc. S5: David Mager. S6: *t.l., t.m.* Michael P. Gadomski/Photo Researchers, Inc.; *t.r.* Gregory K. Scott/Photo Researchers, Inc.; *b.l.* Michael Quintonings/National Geographic Society; *b.m.* Richard Megna/Fundamental Photographs; *b.r.* Paul Silverman/Fundamental Photographs. S7: Culver Pictures. S9: Gary Braasch/Woodfin Camp & Assoc. S10: *b.l.* Michael Quintonings/National Geographic Society. S11: Linde Waidhofer/Liaison International. S12: *l.* Jan Halaska/Photo Researchers, Inc. S14: *t.m.* Richard Hutchings/PhotoEdit; *b.m.* Polecat. S15: Joyce Photographics/Photo Researchers, Inc. S16: *t.r.* Ken N. Johns/Photo Researchers, Inc.; *b.* Sandra Baker/Liaison International. S17: Courtesy Tree Musketeers. **Unit 1** 1: *bkgnd.* Zig Leszczynski/Animals Animals; *inset* Bryan Reinhart/Masterfile. 2: *l.* Allsport/Rick Stewart; *r.* Jerry Wachter/Photo Researchers, Inc. 4: Peter Miller/Photo Researchers, Inc. 5: ©Dick Thomas/VU. 7: ©Jeff J. Daly/VU. 11: *l.* ©Veronika Burmeister/VU; *m.* ©Doug Sokell/VU; *r.* R.M. Meadows/Peter Arnold, Inc. 12: *t.l.* Patrick W. Grace/Science Source/Photo Researchers, Inc.; *b.l.* Gilbert S. Grant/Photo Researchers, Inc.; *l.m.* ©Veronika Burmeister/VU; *r.* ©R. Kessel-G. Shih/VU; *r.m.* ©Cabisco/VU. 13: *t.l.* Phil Degginger/Color-Pic; *b.l.* ©R. Robinson/VU; *t.r.* Blair Seitz/Photo Researchers, Inc.; *b.r.* ©VU. 14: *l.* ©Arthur R. Hill/VU; *r.* ©R.F. Ashley/VU. 16: *l.* Dr. Dennis Kunkel/PhotoTake; *r.* Gregory Ochocki/Photo Researchers, Inc. 17: D.P. Wilson/Eric & David Hosking/Photo Researchers, Inc. 18: *m.l.* ©George Herben/VU; *m.r.* ©Ken Lucas/VU; *b.r.* ©Arthur Morris/VU. 25: G. Buttner/OKAPIA/Photo Researchers, Inc. 26: *l.* ©David S. Addison/VU; *r.* ©Tim Hauf/VU. 27: James R. Holland/National Geographic Society. 28: *bkgnd.* J.C. Teyssier/Publiphoto/Photo Researchers, Inc.; *b.* Tom & Pat Leeson/Photo Researchers, Inc. 30: *l., r.* images copyright ©1998 PhotoDisc, Inc.; *m.* Michael P. Gadomski/Photo Researchers, Inc. 34: ©John Gerlach/VU. 36: ©Jack M. Bostrack/VU. 39: Gerry Ellis/ENP Photography. 40: *bkgnd.* ©Doug Sokell/VU; *b.* Michael P. Gadomski/Photo Researchers, Inc. 41: *t.* ©Ned Therrien/VU; *b.* ©David M. Philips/VU. 42: images copyright ©1998 PhotoDisc, Inc. 43: *bkgnd.* ©TSM/David D. Keaton; *inset* ©TSM/Charles Krebs. 44: ©Tim Hauf/VU. 46: *l.* ©Doug Sokell/VU; *m.* ©John Trager/VU. 47: *l.* ©Bill Beatty/VU; *r.* ©David Sieren/VU; *t.r.* ©Fritz Polking/VU; *b.r.* ©E.F. Anderson/VU. 48: *l.* Dan Suzio/Photo Researchers, Inc. 49: ©David Sieren/VU. 52: ©Dick Keen/VU. 53: George Haling/Photo Researchers, Inc. 56: *l.* Bonnie Sue/Photo Researchers, Inc.; *r.* Peter Skinner/Photo Researchers, Inc. 58: *l.* ©Jim Hughes/VU; *m.* ©VU; *r.* ©Gerald & Buff Corsi/VU. 59: *t.* ©E. Webber/VU; *b.l.* ©John N. Trager/VU; *b.r.* V.P. Weinland/Photo Researchers, Inc. 60: *t.* ©V. McMillan/VU; *b.* ©TSM/Dick Keen. 61: *t.* ©E.F. Anderson/VU; *b.* ©Bud Nielsen/VU. 63: *t.* ©Mark S. Skalny/VU; *b.* ©Arthur R. Hill/VU. 64: *l.* ©John Gerlach/VU; *r.* Jerome Wexler/Photo Researchers, Inc. 65: Alan & Linda Detrick/Photo Researchers, Inc. 66: *bkgnd.* Richard R. Hansen/Photo Researchers, Inc.; Dennis Fagan/Lady Bird Johnson Wildflower Center. 68: *t.* Dr. Jeremy Burgess/Photo Researchers, Inc.; *b.* Gunter Ziesler/Peter Arnold, Inc. 71: *t.* ©Derrick Ditchburn/VU; *m.* ©Doug Sokell/VU; *b.* Adam Jones/Photo Researchers, Inc. 74: R.C. Carpenter/Photo Researchers, Inc. 75: *l.* ©Inga Spence/VU; *m.* ©Ken Wagner/VU; *r.* ©Stephen J. Lang/VU. 79: Kenneth W. Fink/Photo Researchers, Inc. 80: *bkgnd.* Runk/Schoenberger/Grant Heilman Photography, Inc; *t.* Bill Gillette/Stock, Boston; *b.* Jeff Greenberg/PhotoEdit. 81: Emil Muench/Photo Researchers, Inc. 82: *l.* George & Judy Manna/Photo Researchers, Inc.; *r.* ©Mack Henley/VU. 84: ©David Newman/VU. 85: ©R. Calentine/VU. 87: ©Dick Keen/VU. 88: *t.* ©Parke H. John, Jr./VU; *b.* ©Bill Beatty/VU. 89: *b.l.* Steve Kaufman/Peter Arnold, Inc.; *t, b.r.* ©Stan W. Elems/VU. 90: *l.* ©Joe McDonald/VU; *m.* ©Arthur Morris/VU, *r.* ©Barbara Gerlach/VU. 91: Richard T. Nowitz/Corbis. 92: *bkgnd.* Brock May/Photo Researchers, Inc.; *t.* Joel Sartore/Grant Heilman Photography, Inc. **Unit 2** 97: *bkgnd.* ©Paul Chesley/TSI; *inset* images copyright ©1998 PhotoDisc, Inc. 98: *t.* ©Francis/Donna Caldwell/VU; *b.* ©Joe McDonald/VU. 106: *l., m.* Runk/Schoenberger/Grant Heilman Photography, Inc; *r.* ©Yoav Levy/Photo Researchers, Inc. 107: David Waitz. 108: Jay Smith/High and Wild Mt. Guides. 109: NASA/Corbis. 110: SuperStock. 112: Amy C. Etra/PhotoEdit. 115: Tony Freeman/PhotoEdit. 120: ©John Cunningham/VU. 122: *t.* ©A.J. Copley/VU; *m.* ©Henry W. Robison/VU; *b.* ©Mark A. Schneider/VU. 124: *l.* ©D. Cavagnaro/VU; *m.l.* ©W. Banaszewski/VU; *m.r.* ©Mark E. Gibson/VU; *r.* Layne Kennedy/Corbis. 125: Peter Turnley/Corbis. 128: Runk/Schoenberger/Grant Heilman Photography, Inc. 129: ©TSM/Aaron Rezney. 130: *bkgnd.* Digital Stock. 131: Sean Sexton Collection/Corbis. 132: David G. Houser/Corbis. 136: Superstock. 137: ©TSM/Torleif Svensson. 139: NASA. 142: *t.l.* ©Deneve Feigh Bunde/VU; *t.r.* ©Tom Edwards/VU; *b.l.* ©Mark E. Gibson/VU; *b.r.* ©Science VU. 144: *bkgnd.* Carl Purcell/Photo Researchers, Inc. 145: Tiziana and Gianni Baldizzone/Corbis. 147: *bkgnd.* ©Ed Degginger/Bruce Coleman, Inc./PNI; *inset* ©Gene Moore/PhotoTake/PNI. 148: images copyright ©1998 PhotoDisc, Inc. 154: *m.* NASA; *b.l., b.r.* ©1998 AccuWeather, Inc. 155: ©1998 AccuWeather, Inc. 157: ©TSM/David Stoecklei. 158: *b. bkgnd.* NASA; *t.l.* Paul Seheult/Eye Ubiquitous/Corbis; *t.r.* images copyright ©1998 PhotoDisc, Inc.; *b.r.* Corbis-Bettmann. 159: *t.l.* National Weather Service/AP/Wide World; *t.r.* NASA/AP/Wide World. 160: ©VU. 163: ©Nada Pencik/VU. 165: ©Gene Moore/PhotoTake. 167: ©Science VU. 168: Carlos Guerrero. 169: *bkgnd.* ©Marc Epstein/VU; *inset* ©Mark A. Schneider/VU. 170: *bkgnd.* ©R.F. Meyers/VU. 172: *t.* Keith Kent/Peter Arnold, Inc.; *b.* ©NOAA/Peter Arnold, Inc. 173: Carlos Guerrero. 176: *t.l.* ©TSM/Carlos Humberto; *t.r.* ©Martin G. Miller/VU; *b.l.* ©TSM/Strauss/Curtis; *b.r.* ©TSM/Torleif Svensson. 184: *l.* ©Science VU; *r.* ©VU. 185: Steve Kaufman/Peter Arnold, Inc. 186: *t.* ©Don Smetzer/TSI; *b.* Jeff Greenberg/PhotoEdit. 187: Abraham Hondius/Bridgeman Art Library Intl. Ltd. **Unit 3** 193: Ezio Geneletti/The Image Bank. 194: ©TSM/Photri. 196: Daemmrich/The Image Works. 197: ©Artville LLC 1997. 198: Macmillan/McGraw-Hill School Division. 200: ©Ken Fisher/TSI. 201: ©TSM/Norbert Wu. 203: ©TSM/Ed Bock. 204: *l.* National Geographic photographer Chris Johns; *r.* Michael A. Hampshire. 205: H. Edward Kim. 206: S. Tanaka/The Picture Cube. 208: ©Artville LLC 1997; *inset* images copyright ©1998 PhotoDisc, Inc. 209: Tim Davis/Photo Researchers, Inc. 210: *r.* Michael Krasowitz/FPG; *l.* Courtesy Alexander Graham Bell National Historic Park. 211: George Hall/Corbis. 213: ©TSM/Tibor Bognar. 214: images copyright ©1998 PhotoDisc, Inc. 215: Dr. Jeremy Burgess/Photo Researchers, Inc. 216: Brenda Tharp/Photo Researchers, Inc. 218: Gary Gold/Gamma-Liaison. 220: Allsport/Brian Bahr. 221: *l.* ©Marty Loken/TSI; *r.* Museum der Stadt, Vienna, Austria/Superstock. 222: *l.* Macmillan/McGraw-Hill School Division; *r.* ©TSM/John M. Roberts. 223: Wolfgang Kaehler/Corbis. 226: Joseph Schuyler/Stock, Boston. 227: Luc Novovitch/Gamma-Liaison. 231: Carr Clifton. 232: ©John Elk/TSI. 234: *t.* ©Arthur Morris/VU; *b.* Robert Holmgren/Peter Arnold, Inc. 235: ©TSM/Pete Saloutos. 236: *l.* ©Barb Gerlach/VU; *m.* ©Rich Treptow/VU; *r.* ©C.P. George/VU. 237: *t.* ©Science VU; *m.* ©Jeff Daly/VU; *b.r.* ©Cabisco/VU. 239: Barry B. Luokkala/Department of Physics, Carnegie Mellon University. 242, 243: Roger Ressmeyer/Corbis. 244: Cesar Llacuna. 245: McGraw-Hill School Division. 246: *bkgnd.* Wolfgang Kaehler/Corbis; *l.* Science Photo Library/Photo Researchers, Inc.; *r.* North Wind. 247: *l.* The Queens Borough Public Library, Long Island Division, Latimer Family Papers; *r.* Hall of Electricital History, Schenectady Museum, Schenectady, New York. 248: Kevin Fleming/Corbis. 250: *t.* ©Science VU. 251: *r.* ©Jeff Greenberg/VU. 252: *t.* ©Bill Beatty/VU. 258: ©James Webb/PhotoTake. 259: Bob Rowan/Progressive Images/Corbis. 267: Macmillan/McGraw-Hill School Division. 269: Allsport/Mike Powell. 272: ©Science VU. 276: Corbis-Bettmann. 278: *l.* Joseph Sohm/ChromoSohm, Inc./Corbis; *r.* ©Mark E. Gibson/VU. 279: *b.* ©Science VU; *t.* images copyright ©1998 PhotoDisc, Inc. 280: Macmillan/McGraw-Hill School Division. 281: *t.* Dr. Mony de Leon/Peter Arnold, Inc.; *l.* ©John D. Cunningham/VU; *b.* Doug Martin/Photo Researchers, Inc. 282: ©Science VU. 283: Macmillan/McGraw-Hill School Division. 284: *bkgnd.* Hulton-Deutsch Collection/Corbis. **Unit 4** 289: *bkgnd.* ©Yoav Levy/PhotoTake; *inset* images copyright ©1998 PhotoDisc. 290: Jonathon Blair/Corbis. 297: *t.l.* Klaus Guldbrandsen/Science Photo Library/Photo Researchers, Inc.; *t.r.* George Bernard/Photo Researchers, Inc.; *m.l.* The Purcell Team/Corbis; *m.r.* Vaughan Fleming/Science Photo Library/Photo Researchers, Inc.; *b.l.* Buddy Mays/Corbis; *b.r.* Wolfgang Kaehler/Corbis. 299: Walter Meayers Edwards. 300: *m., b.* Phil Degginger/Color-Pic, Inc. 302: *t.* IBM Research/Peter Arnold, Inc.; *b.* ©National Railway of Japan/PhotoTake. 303: images copyright ©1998 PhotoDisc, Inc. 304, 305: Stephen Frink/Southern Stock/PNI. 306: NASA. 308: *t.* Lowell Georgia/Photo Researchers, Inc.; *b.* Rich Treptow/Photo Researchers, Inc. 309: *t.l.* ©Science/VU; *t.r., m., b.l., b.r.* Charles D. Winters/Photo Researchers, Inc.; *m.l.* Russ Lappa/Science Source/Photo Researchers, Inc. 310: *t.l.* Runk/Schoenberger/Grant Heilman Photography, Inc.; *f.b.r.* ©Bill Beatty/VU; *b.m.* ©Yoav Levy/PhotoTake; *b.l.* & *b.r.* images copyright ©1998 PhotoDisc, Inc. 311: David Taylor/Photo Researchers, Inc. 312: *t.* IBM Research/Peter Arnold, Inc.; *b.* ©Science VU/BMRL. 314: *f.t.l., f.t.r.* E.R. Degginger/Color-Pic, Inc.; *t.l.* George Bernard/Photo Researchers, Inc.; *t.m., t.r.* Klaus Guldbrandsen/Photo Researchers, Inc.; *m.* Rich Treptow/Photo Researchers, Inc.; *b.l.* Charles D. Winters/Photo Researchers, Inc.; *b.r.* Russ Lappa/Photo Researchers, Inc. 318: *t.l.* Christine Coscioni/CO2, Inc; *t.r.* Leonard Lessin/Peter Arnold, Inc.; *b.l.* ©API/VU. 319: Christine Coscioni/CO2, Inc. 320: *l.* ©Gilbert L. Twiest/VU; *r.* Joe Sohm/Chromosohm/Stock, Boston. 321: *bkgnd.* images copyright ©1998 PhotoDisc, Inc.; *t.l. inset* The Granger Collection; *t.r. inset* Corbis-Bettmann. 322: ©Javier Domingo/PhotoTake. 324: *l.* Gordon Wiltsie/Peter Arnold, Inc.; *m.* Clyde H. Smith/Peter Arnold, Inc.; *r.* Jeff & Alexa Henry/Peter Arnold, Inc. 325: Cesar Llacuna. 328: *t.* ©Jakub Jasinski/VU; *b.l.* ©Kjell B. Sandved/VU; *b.r.* Darrell Gulin/Corbis. 330: *t.l.* ©Carolina Biological Supply/PhotoTake; *t.r.* Cesar Llacuna; *m.* Christine L. Coscioni/CO2, Inc; *b.* Charles D. Winters/Photo Researchers, Inc. 332: *t.* ©TSM/Mugshots; *b.* ©TSM/Chris Rogers. 333: Richard Choy/Peter Arnold, Inc. 334: Rod Plack/Photo Researchers, Inc. 337: ©TSM/Mark M. Lawrence. 338: *l.* Mark Marten/Science Source/Photo Researchers, Inc.; *r.* Alex S. MacLean/Peter Arnold, Inc. 340: *r.* Jacana/Photo Researchers, Inc. 344: *t.* Charles D.

Winters/Photo Researchers, Inc. 345: *t.r.* Gordon Wiltsie/Peter Arnold, Inc.; *b.* ©Artville LLC 1997. 346: *t.* M.I. Walker/Photo Researchers, Inc.; *b.* ©S. Strickland/Naturescapes/VU. 348: *t.* ©SIU/VU; *b.* ©Mark E. Gibson/VU. 350: Larry Lefever/Grant Heilman Photography, Inc. 351: *t.* ©David S. Addison/VU; *b.* David R. Frazier/Photo Researchers, Inc. 352: *l.* NASA; *r.* ©Doug Sokell/VU. 355: *b.l.* Phil Degginger/Color-Pic, Inc.; *b.r.* ©A.J. Copley/VU. 357: *t.* Christine Coscioni/CO2, Inc; *b.* Cesar Llacuna. 359: Lee Snyder/Photo Researchers, Inc. 360: *l.* NASA; *m.* Christine L. Coscioni/CO2, Inc.; *inset* ©Science/VU; *r. inset* Leonard Lessin/Peter Arnold, Inc. 362: *t.* ©TSM/Roger Ball; *b.* ©Science/VU. 363: Craig Lovell/Corbis. 365: *l.* ©John D. Cunningham/VU; *r.* Geoff Bryant/Photo Researchers, Inc. 366: Jeff Rotman. 368: E.R. Degginger/Color-Pic, Inc. 369: *l.* Leonard Lessin/Peter Arnold, Inc. 371: Ed Young/Corbis. 373: *r.* images copyright ©1998 PhotoDisc, Inc. 374: *l.* Andrew McClenaghan/Photo Researchers, Inc.; *r.* ©Science/VU. 375: *l.* Richard Hamilton Smith/Corbis. 378: Runk/Schoenberger/Grant Heilman Photography, Inc. **Unit 5** 385: *inset* ©Nathan Bilow/TSI; *bkgnd.* ©Ralf Gerard/TSI. 386: ©NASA/PhotoTake. 387: McGraw-Hill School Division. 390: *t.* Blocker Collections/UT Medical Branch. 391: Mehau Kulyk/Photo Researchers, Inc. 396: *t.* World Perspectives/Explorer/Photo Researchers, Inc.; *b.l., b.r. bkgnd.* NASA; *b.* ©Science/VU. 397: Jim Zipp/Photo Researchers, Inc. 398: *t.l, t.r.* NASA/JPL/Caltech; *b.l.* NASA; *b.r.* NASA/JPL. 400: *l.* ©Science/VU; *r.* David Parker/Science Photo Library/Photo Researchers, Inc. 402: *l.* Sinclair Stammers/Science Photo Library/Photo Researchers, Inc.; *r.* ©John D. Cunningham/VU. 405: *l.* Dr. E.R. Degginger/Color-Pic, Inc.; *r.* ©Stella Snead/Bruce Coleman, Inc. 406: *l.* Jerry Schad/Photo Researchers, Inc.; *m.* Robert Godwin/National Audubon Society/Photo Researchers, Inc.; *r.* Jim Steinberg/Photo Researchers, Inc. 407: *t.* ©Steve McCutcheon/VU; *b.* Gilbert Grant/Photo Researchers, Inc. 408: *l.* Renee Lynn/Photo Researchers, Inc.; *r.* ©Albert J. Copley/VU. 409: Terranova International/Photo Researchers, Inc. 410: *t.* David Scharf/Peter Arnold, Inc.; *m.* Bruce Coleman, Inc.; *b.* ©NASA/PhotoTake. 411: NASA/Science Photo Library/Photo Researchers, Inc. 412: *bkgnd.* Dave Bartruff/Stock, Boston; *b.* ©Mark Mellett/Stock, Boston. 413: *l.* Annie Griffiths Belt/Corbis; *r.* Morton Beebe-S.F./Corbis. 414: *l.* Joyce Photographics/Photo Researchers, Inc.; *r.* Tom McHugh/Photo Researchers, Inc. 416: *t.l.* Joyce Photographics/Photo Researchers, Inc.; *m.l.* E.R. Degginger/Photo Researchers, Inc.; *b.l.* Cesar Llacuna; *m.* Charles D. Winters/Timeframe Photography, Inc./Photo Researchers, Inc.; *r.* George Whiteley/Photo Researchers, Inc. 417: *t.l.* Roberto De Gugliemo/Science Photo Library/Photo Researchers, Inc.; *m.l.* Kaj R. Svensson/Science Photo Library/Photo Researchers, Inc.; *m.r.* J.H. Robinson/Photo Researchers, Inc.; *b.* Cesar Llacuna. 418: *t.l.* ©John D. Cunningham/VU; *m.* ©Mark A. Schneider/VU; *b.l.* ©Tom Pantages/PhotoTake. 419: ©A.J. Cunningham/VU. 420: *bkgnd.* Charles O'Rear/Corbis; *t.l.* ©Ross Frid/Korner Gems, Traverse City, MI/VU; *t.r.* Joyce Photographics/Photo Researchers, Inc.; *b.* ©A.J. Copley/VU. 421: Peter Aitken/Photo Researchers, Inc. 422: *t.l.* ©LINK/VU; *t.r.* Richard T. Nowitz/Photo Researchers, Inc.; *b.l.* ©A.J. Copley/VU; *b.r.* ©Zale Corporation. 423: Michael W. Davidson/Photo Researchers, Inc. 424: *bkgnd., b.r.* Hulton-Getty/Liaison Agency; *b.l.* ©Ron Sanford/TSI. 425: *b.* ©Jim Simmen/TSI; *t.* Dave G. Houser/Corbis. 426: *l.* ©Dick Keen/VU; *r.* E.R. Degginger/Photo Researchers, Inc. 428: *bkgnd.* Owen Franken/Corbis; *t.l., m.l.* E.R. Degginger/Photo Researchers, Inc.; *r.* Biophoto Associates/Photo Researchers, Inc. 429: *t.l., b.* Andrew J. Martinez/Photo Researchers, Inc.; *t.r.* ©Doug Sokell/VU. 430: *t.* Andrew J. Martinez/Photo Researchers, Inc.; *m.* ©Martin G. Miller/VU; *b.m.* Joyce Photographics/Photo Researchers, Inc.; *b.* ©A.J. Copley/VU. 431: *t.l.* Kjell B. Sandved/Photo Researchers, Inc.; *b.l.* Joyce Photographics/Photo Researchers, Inc.; *r.* ©John D. Cunningham/VU. 432: *t.l.* ©Arthur R. Hill/VU; *t.r.* ©L.S. Stepanowicz/VU; *b.l.* E.R. Degginger/Photo Researchers, Inc.; *b.r.* Charles R. Belinky/Photo Researchers, Inc. 433: Michael P. Gadomski/Photo Researchers, Inc. 434: Joyce Photographics/Photo Researchers, Inc. 436: G. Byttner Naturbild/OKAPIA/Photo Researchers, Inc. 437: *l.* ©Ron Spomer/VU; *r.* Christian Grzimek/OKAPIA/Photo Researchers, Inc. 439: Spencer Grant/Photo Researchers, Inc. 440: *bkgnd.* ©Thomas Del Grase/TSI; *b.* North Wind Pictures. 441: *t.* Richard Hutchings/PhotoEdit; *b.l.* Hulton-Getty/Liaison Agency; *b.r.* North Wind Pictures. 443: *inset* ©Keith Wood/TSI; *bkgnd.* ©Terry Vine/TSI. 444: *l.* Will & Deni McIntyre/Photo Researchers, Inc.; *r.* Tom McHugh/Photo Researchers, Inc. 446: images copyright ©1998 PhotoDisc, Inc. 448: *l.* Phil Degginger/Color-Pic, Inc.; *m.* Hattie Young/Science Photo Library/Photo Researchers, Inc.; *r.* ©Gary Withey/Bruce Coleman, Inc. 449: Simon Fraser/Science Photo Library/Photo Researchers, Inc. 451: *l.* NASA/Science Photo Library/Photo Researchers, Inc.; *r.* NASA/Photo Researchers, Inc. 452: *t.* NASA/Digital Stock; *m.* NASA; *b.* JPL/NASA. 453: *t.l.* NASA; *t.r.* NASA/Photo Researchers, Inc. 454: IFA/Peter Arnold, Inc. 457: *l.* Calvin Larsen/Photo Researchers, Inc.; *r.* Simon Fraser/Science Photo Library/Photo Researchers, Inc. 460: Simon Fraser/Science Photo Library/Photo Researchers, Inc. 463: David M. Grossman/Photo Researchers, Inc. 464: *bkgnd.* Martin Dohrn/Science Photo Library/Photo Researchers, Inc.; Courtesy SAWS. 466: Jeff Isaac Greenberg/Photo Researchers, Inc. 468: *l.* Phil Degginger/Color-Pic, Inc.; *r.* Joseph Nettis/Photo Researchers, Inc. 469: Ted Speigel/Corbis. 472: *l.* Phil Degginger/Color-Pic, Inc.; *m.* Russell D. Curtis/Photo Researchers, Inc.; *r.* Simon Fraser/Science Photo Library/Photo Researchers, Inc. 473: *l.* John Keating/Photo Researchers, Inc.; *r.* Kevin Schafer/Peter Arnold, Inc. 474: Patrick Grace/Photo Researchers, Inc. 475: J. Greenberg/Peter Arnold, Inc. 476: *bkgnd.* Grant Heilman Photography, Inc.; *l.* ©Bruce Forster/TSI. 480: NASA. **Unit 6** 481: *bkgnd.* ©Ken Wagner/PhotoTake/PNI; *inset* Steve Hopkin/Masterfile. 482: *l.* ©J. McDonald/Bruce Coleman, Inc.; *r.* ©Danilo G. Donadoni/Bruce Coleman, Inc. 486: ©John Shaw/Bruce Coleman, Inc. 487: ©Scott Berner/VU. 488: ©Lee Rentz/Bruce Coleman, Inc. 489: *t.* ©Laura Riley/Bruce Coleman, Inc.; *b.* ©Joe McDonald/Bruce Coleman, Inc. 490: ©Bruce Coleman, Inc. 491: *t.* Digital Stock; *b.* ©N.E. Swedberg/Bruce Coleman, Inc. 492: ©John Shaw/Bruce Coleman, Inc. 493: Richard Hamilton Smith/Corbis. 494: *t.* Gordon Wiltsie; *b.* Maria Stenzel. 495: Tom Van Sant, Geosphere Project/Planetary Visions/SPL/Photo Researchers, Inc. 496: Breck P. Kent/Animals Animals; 499: images copyright ©1998 PhotoDisc, Inc. 502: *t.* Scott Smith/Animals Animals; *b.* Robert F. Sisson. 503: *t.* ©Doug Wechsler/Animals Animals; *b.* ©Bruce Coleman, Inc. 506: *l.* John Pontier/Animals Animals; *r.* Carson Baldwin, Jr./Animals Animals. 507: Zig Leszczynski/Animals Animals. 508: *bkgnd.* Porterfield-Chickering/Photo Researchers, Inc. 509: *t.l.* ©Jeff Greenberg/VU; *t.r.* Larry Lefever/Grant Heilman Photography, Inc.; *m.* Jim Sugar Photography/Corbis. 510: *t.* ©Bill Ruth/Bruce Coleman, Inc.; *b.* ©John S. Flannery/Bruce Coleman, Inc. 512: ©Jack W. Dyking/Bruce Coleman, Inc. 513: *t.* Zig Leszczynski/Earth Scenes; *b.* Breck P. Kent/Earth Scenes. 514: F.R. Degginger/Earth Scenes. 515: Cesar Llacuna. 521: ©TSM/Peter Beck. 522: *bkgnd.* Photo Library International/ESA/Photo Researchers, Inc. 523: *t.* Lowell Georgia/Photo Researchers, Inc.; *b.* Runk/Schoenberger/Grant Heilman Photography, Inc. 524: images copyright ©1998 PhotoDisc, Inc. 525: *inset* ©TSM/ZEFA HUMMEL; *bkgnd.* ©TSM/ZEFA GERMANY. 526: *t.* ©John Elk/Bruce Coleman, Inc.; *b.* ©Frank Krahmer/Bruce Coleman, Inc. 528: *l.* ©John Shaw/Bruce Coleman, Inc.; *r.* ©B&C Calhoun/Bruce Coleman, Inc. 529: *l.* ©Jeff Foott/Bruce Coleman, Inc. 530: Patti Murray/Earth Scenes. 531: Linda Bailery/Earth Scenes. 532: ©Mark Newman/Bruce Coleman, Inc. 533: ©M.P.L. Fogden/Bruce Coleman, Inc. 534: *t.l.* ©David Overcash/Bruce Coleman, Inc.; *t.r.* ©John Shaw/Bruce Coleman, Inc.; *b.l.* images copyright ©1998 PhotoDisc, Inc.; *b.r.* E.R. Degginger/Animals Animals. 535: *t.* Gregory Brown/Animals Animals, *b.* ©Patty Murray/Earth Scenes. 536: ©D&M Plage/Bruce Coleman, Inc. 538: *t.* ©Rod Williams/Bruce Coleman, Inc.; *b.* Kevin Schafer/Corbis. 539: ©David Madison/Bruce Coleman, Inc. 540: *bkgnd.* SCIMAT/Photo Researchers, Inc.; *l.* Mary Steinbacher/PhotoEdit. 541: Cesar Llacuna. 542: *l.* Patti Murray/Earth Scenes; *r.* ©Ken Graham/Bruce Coleman, Inc. 544: *t.* Breck P. Kent/Earth Scenes; *m.* ©Lee Rentz/Rentl/Bruce Coleman, Inc.; *b.* Nigel J.H. Smith/Earth Scenes. 545: *t.* ©J.C. Carton/Bruce Coleman, Inc.; *m.* Eastcott/Momatiuk/Earth Scenes; *b.* ©M. Timothy O'Keefe/Bruce Coleman, Inc. 546: A.&M. Shah/Animals Animals. 547: Eastcott/Momatiuk/Earth Scenes. 548: *l.* ©Joe McDonald/Bruce Coleman, Inc.; *r.* ©Joy Spurr/Bruce Coleman, Inc. 549: *t.* ©John Shaw/Bruce Coleman, Inc.; *m.* ©Jen & Des Bartlett/Bruce Coleman, Inc.; *b.* ©Jeff Foott/Bruce Coleman, Inc. 551: *t.* Jim Tuten/Animals Animals; *b.* ©E&P Bauer/Bruce Coleman, Inc. 552: images copyright ©1998 PhotoDisc, Inc. 554: Steve McCutcheon/AllStock/PNI. 555: ©N. Devore III/Bruce Coleman, Inc. 556: *bkgnd.* ©Jacques Jangoux/TSI; *l.* ©John D. Cunningham/VU. 558: Jim Sugar Photography/Corbis. 559: Breck P. Kent/Earth Scenes. 560: ©John Elk III/Bruce Coleman, Inc. 562: *l.* Patti Murray/Earth Scenes; *r.* ©David Falconer/Bruce Coleman, Inc. 563: John Lemker/Earth Scenes. 565: *l.* E.R. Degginger/Earth Scenes; *t.r.* images copyright ©1998 PhotoDisc, Inc. 566: *t.r.* ©S. Jonasson/Bruce Coleman, Inc.; *m.* E.R. Degginger/Earth Scenes; *b.* Krafft/Explorer/Photo Researchers, Inc. 568: images copyright ©1998 PhotoDisc, Inc. 570: ©John H. Hoffman/Bruce Coleman, Inc. 571: Jeff Greenberg/Photo Researchers, Inc. 572: *bkgnd.* David Ulmer/Stock, Boston; Courtesy Mickey Burleson. **Unit 7** 577: Superstock. 578: Michael Newman/PhotoEdit. 579: Cesar Llacuna. 580: *l.* Superstock; *r.* ©Fred Hossler/VU. 581: The Granger Collection. 582: VideoSurgery/Photo Researchers, Inc. 584: David R. Frazier Photolibrary/Photo Researchers, Inc. 586: *t.* Meckes/Ottawa/Photo Researchers, Inc.; *b.* Biophoto Associates/Photo Researchers, Inc. 587: Bob Daemmrich/Daemmrich Photography. 588: Rudi Von Briel/PhotoEdit. 589: Meckes/Ottawa/Photo Researchers, Inc. 590: *l.* ©Paul Chesley/TSI; *r.* Keren Su/Stock, Boston. 594: *t.* Mary Kate Denny/PhotoEdit; *b.* John Kaprielian/Photo Researchers, Inc. 596: *t.r.* Bob Daemmrich/Stock, Boston; *b.l.* Mary Steinbacher/PhotoEdit. 597: *l.* images copyright ©1998 PhotoDisc, Inc.; *r.* John Bavosi/Science Photo Library/Photo Researchers, Inc. 598: Biophoto Associates/Photo Researchers, Inc. 599: *t.r.* ©John Millar/TSI; *b.l.* Cimitri Lundt/Temport/Corbis. 601: ©TSM/Chris Hamilton. 602: Kenneth Chen/Envision. 605: Cesar Llacuna. 609: Michael Newman/PhotoEdit. 610: Phyllis Picardi/Stock, Boston. 611: Michael Newman/PhotoEdit. 612: *t.* SIU/Photo Researchers, Inc.; *b.* Martin M. Rotker/Science Source/Photo Researchers, Inc. 614: *l.* images copyright ©1998 PhotoDisc, Inc.; *r.* Allsport/Vincent Laforet. 615: *t.* Jean Marc Barey/Photo Researchers, Inc.; *m.* Bob Daemmrich/Stock, Boston; *m.r.* images copyright ©1998 PhotoDisc, Inc.; *b.l.* David Young-Wolff/PhotoEdit; *b.m.* Bob Daemmrich/Stock, Boston; *b.r.* ©Mark E.Gibson/VU. 616: *t.l.* Rafael Macia/Photo Researchers, Inc.; *t.r.* Bob Daemmrich/Stock, Boston; *b.* Tim Davis/Photo Researchers, Inc. 619: Bonnie Kamin/PhotoEdit. 620: *t.l.* David Madison/TSI; *b.l.* Tim Davis/Photo Researchers, Inc.; *r.* Lawrence Migdale/Stock, Boston. R9: *r.* NASA/Digital Stock. R10: images copyright ©1998 PhotoDisc. R16: *t.r.* Jim Harrison/Stock, Boston/PNI. R20: *t.* UCO/Lick Observatory Photo/Image; *m.* Camerique/H.A. Roberts, Inc. R24: *b. bkgnd.* images copyright ©1998 PhotoDisc; *b. inset* G.R. Roberts/Photo Researchers, Inc. R25: *b. inset* ©1998 AccuWeather, Inc.